Town Life in A

Richard Ernest Nowell Twopeny

Alpha Editions

This edition published in 2024

ISBN : 9789357965446

Design and Setting By
Alpha Editions
www.alphaedis.com
Email - info@alphaedis.com

As per information held with us this book is in Public Domain.
This book is a reproduction of an important historical work. Alpha Editions uses the best technology to reproduce historical work in the same manner it was first published to preserve its original nature. Any marks or number seen are left intentionally to preserve its true form.

Contents

A WALK ROUND MELBOURNE	- 1 -
SYDNEY.	- 11 -
ADELAIDE.	- 15 -
HOUSES.	- 18 -
FURNITURE.	- 23 -
SERVANTS.	- 30 -
FOOD.	- 38 -
DRESS.	- 45 -
YOUNG AUSTRALIA.	- 50 -
SOCIAL RELATIONS.	- 61 -
RELIGION AND MORALS.	- 68 -
EDUCATION.	- 76 -
POLITICS.	- 88 -
BUSINESS.	- 110 -
SHOPS.	- 116 -
AMUSEMENTS.	- 118 -
NEWSPAPERS.	- 129 -
LITERATURE, LANGUAGE, AND ART.	- 141 -

A WALK ROUND MELBOURNE.

Although most educated people know that Melbourne, Sydney, and Adelaide are populous towns, I should doubt whether one Englishman, who has not been to Australia, out of a hundred *realizes* that fact. I well remember that, although I had taken some trouble to read up information about Melbourne, I was never more thoroughly surprised than during the first few hours after my arrival there. And I hear almost everyone who comes out from England say that his experience has been the same as my own. In one sense the visitor is disappointed with his first day in an Australian city. The novelties and the differences from the Old Country do not strike him nearly so much as the resemblances. It is only as he gets to know the place better that he begins to to notice the differences. The first prevailing impression is that a slice of Liverpool has been bodily transplanted to the Antipodes, that you must have landed in England again by mistake, and it is only by degrees that you begin to see that the resemblance is more superficial than real.

Although Sydney is the older town, Melbourne is justly entitled to be considered the metropolis of the Southern Hemisphere. The natural beauties of Sydney are worth coming all the way to Australia to see; while the situation of Melbourne is commonplace if not actually ugly; but it is in the Victorian city that the trade and capital, the business and pleasure of Australia chiefly centre. Is there a company to be got up to stock the wilds of Western Australia, or to form a railway on the land-grant system in Queensland, to introduce the electric light, or to spread education amongst the black fellows, the promoters either belong to Melbourne, or go there for their capital. The headquarters of nearly all the large commercial institutions which extend their operation beyond the limits of any one colony are to be found there. If you wish to transact business well and quickly, to organize a new enterprise--in short, to estimate and understand the trade of Australia, you must go to Melbourne and not to Sydney, and this in spite of the fact that Victoria is a small colony handicapped by heavy protectionist duties, whilst Sydney is, comparatively speaking, a free port, at the base of an enormous area. The actual production does not take place in Victoria, but it is in Melbourne that the money resulting from the productions of other colonies as well as of Victoria is turned over. It is Melbourne money chiefly that opens up new tracts of land for settlement in the interior of the continent, and Melbourne brains that find the outlets for fresh commerce in every direction. There is a bustle and life about Melbourne which you altogether miss in Sydney. The Melbourne man is always on the look-out for business, the Sydney man waits for business to come to him. The one is always in a hurry, the other takes life more easily. And as it is with business, so it is with pleasure.

If you are a man of leisure you will find more society in Melbourne, more balls and parties, a larger measure of intellectual life--i.e., more books and men of education and intellect, more and better theatrical and musical performances, more racing and cricket, football, and athletic clubs, a larger leisured class than in Sydney. The bushman who comes to town to 'knock down his cheque,' the squatter who wants a little amusement, both prefer Melbourne to spend their money in. The Melbourne races attract three or four times the number of visitors that the Sydney races do; all public amusements are far better attended in Melbourne; the people dress better, talk better, think better, are better, if we accept Herbert Spencer's definition of Progress. There is far more 'go' and far more 'life,' in every sense of these rather comprehensive words, to be found in Melbourne, and it is there that the visitor must come who wishes to see the fullest development of Australasian civilisation, whether in commerce or education, in wealth or intellect, in manners and customs--in short, in every department of life.

If you ask how this anomaly is to be explained, I can only answer that the shutting out of Sydney from the country behind it by a barrier of mountains hindered its early development; whilst the gold-diggings transformed Melbourne from a village into a city almost by magic; that the first population of Sydney was of the wrong sort, whilst that which flooded Melbourne from 1851 to 1861 was eminently adventurous and enterprising; that Melbourne having achieved the premier position, Sydney has, with all its later advantages, found the truth of the proverbs: 'A stern chase is a long chase,' and 'To him that hath shall be given.'

Passengers by ocean-going vessels to Melbourne land either at Sandridge or Williamstown, small shipping towns situated on either side of the river Yarra, which is only navigable by the smaller craft. A quarter of an hour in the train brings the visitor into the heart of the city. On getting out he can hardly fail to be impressed by the size of the buildings around him, and by the width of the streets, which are laid out in rectangular blocks, the footpaths being all well paved or asphalted. In spite of the abundance of large and fine-looking buildings, there is a rather higgledy-piggledy look about the town--the city you will by this time own it to be. There are no building laws, and every man has built as seemed best in his own eyes. The town is constantly outgrowing the majority of its buildings, and although the wise plan of allowing for the rapid growth of a young community, and building for the requirements of the future rather than of the present, is generally observed, there are still gaps in the line of the streets towards the outskirts, and houses remaining which were built by unbelievers in the future before the city. In the main thoroughfares you might fancy yourself in an improved Edgeware Road. In a few years Collins and Bourke Streets will be very like Westbourne Grove. The less frequented streets in the city are like those of London suburbs. There *are* a few lanes which it is wiser not to go down after ten o'clock at night. These are known as the back slums. But nowhere is there any sign of poverty or anything at all resembling Stepney or the lower parts of an European city, The Chinese quarter is the nearest approach thereto, but it is quite *sui generis*, and squalor is altogether absent.

The town is well lighted with gas, and the water-supply, from reservoirs on the Yarra a few miles above, is plentiful, but not good for drinking. There Is no underground drainage system. All the sewage is carried away in huge open gutters, which run all through the town, and are at their worst and widest in the most central part, where all the principal shops and business places are situated. These gutters are crossed by little wooden bridges every fifty yards. When it rains, they rise to the proportion of small torrents, and have on several occasions proved fatal to drunken men. In one heavy storm, indeed, a sober strong man was carried off his legs by the force of the stream, and ignominiously drowned in a gutter. You may imagine how unpleasant these little rivers are to carriage folk. In compensation they are as yet untroubled with tramways, although another couple of years will probably see rails laid all over the city.

It is a law in every Australian town that no visitor shall be allowed to rest until he has seen all its sights, done all its lions, and, above all, expressed his surprise and admiration at them. With regard to their public institutions, the colonists are like children with a new toy--delighted with it themselves, and not contented until everybody they meet has declared it to be delightful. There are some people who vote all sightseeing a bore, but if they come to Melbourne I would advise them at least to do the last part of their duty-- express loudly and generally their admiration at everything that is mentioned to them. Whether they have seen it or not is, after all, their own affair.

In this respect a Professor at the Melbourne University, on a holiday trip to New Zealand, has just told me an amusing anecdote, for the literal truth of which he vouches. A couple of young Englishmen fresh from Oxford came to Melbourne in the course of a trip round the world to open up their minds! For fear of a libel suit I may at once say I am not alluding to the Messrs. Chamberlain. They brought letters of introduction to Professor S----, who proposed, according to the custom of the place, to 'show them round.' 'Have you seen the Public Library?' he began. 'No,' answered the Oxonian. Shall I take you over it?' continued the Professor; 'it is one of the finest in the world, well worth seeing; and we can kill two birds with one stone by seeing the Museum and National Gallery at the same time.' 'Well, no, thanks,' was the reply; 'it's awfully good of you, we know; but I say, the fact is books are books, all the world over, and pictures are pictures; and as for minerals, I can't say we understand them--not in our line, you understand.'

The Professor now thought he would try them with something out-of-doors, and proposed a walk to the Botanical Gardens, which was met with 'Don't you think it's rather hot for a walk? Besides, to tell the truth, one garden is very much like another.' 'But these are very large,' persisted the Professor; 'not scientific gardens like Kew, but capital places to walk and sit about in. There are a number of flowers there, too, which you cannot see at home.' Oxonian No. 2, however, came to the breach: 'We bought a lot of flowers at a shop in Collins Street yesterday, and we are going to send a hamper of ferns home; so that if you won't think it uncivil of us to refuse your kindness, we won't take up your time by going so far.'

Although somewhat abashed, the Professor thought of several other 'lions' which they might like to see, but was invariably met with the same polite refusal, till at last he gave it up as a bad job, and turned the conversation to general subjects. They had taken up their hats, and were saying good-bye. The Professor, who is a kind-hearted man, and was really anxious to be of service to the two friends, felt quite vexed with himself that he could do nothing more than ask them to dine. So, just as they were parting with the usual mutual expressions of goodwill, he asked in a despondent, almost prayerful tone: 'Are you quite sure there is; nothing I can do for you? Pray make use of me if you can, and I shall be only too delighted.' The reply was in a rather nervous voice from the younger man, who blushed as he asked the favour: 'Do you know anyone who has got a lawn-tennis court? We should so awfully like to have a game.'

The Professor introduced them to the head and to some of the undergraduates of the affiliated colleges close by, and heard very little more of them till they came to dinner with him a fortnight later, the day before they were to leave Melbourne. The conversation at dinner turned of course upon what they had seen during their visit, with which they declared themselves immensely pleased. But when asked as to the things which had most impressed them, it came out that Sundays were the only days they had gone out of the town; that they had not been to see a public institution or building, except their bank and the theatres. 'Surely you can't have spent all your time at the club,' said the Professor, 'though there is a capital library there; and, by the way, did you ever play tennis at Ormond College?' And then came the reply from both at once. It turned out that they had been to Ormond College to play tennis twice a day, except when they stopped lunch there. And then followed a technical description of the college tennis-courts, the Australian play, etc., etc.

But the cream of the story is not yet reached. The young men were to leave the next day for Japan, and the Professor waxed enthusiastic over the delights in store for them in that land of the morning. He quoted anecdotes and passages from Miss Bird's book, and repeated more than once that he envied them their trip. 'Well, yes, you know,' said the eldest, 'we've got several introductions; and I hear there are lots of English in Tokio, so that we are sure to get plenty of tennis.'

There are not many people who are likely to be so frank, not to say dull, as the Professor's friends; but how many people there are who travel round the world and see nothing! There is a moral in the story which is probably applicable to at least half of my readers, more or less.

Of the public buildings, which are scattered in considerable numbers about the town, the largest are the New Law Courts, which have just been erected at a cost of £300,000. They contain 130 rooms, and provide accommodation for the Supreme Court, the County Court, the Insolvent Court, the Equity Court, and for the various offices of the Crown Law Department. The plan is that of a quadrangle, with a centre surmounted by a dome 137 feet high. Still more elaborate and magnificent are the Parliament Houses not yet completed, the front alone of which is to cost £180,000. With regard to the architecture of these buildings, there is ample room for difference of opinion, but everyone will agree to admire the classic simplicity of the Public Library, erected some twenty years ago, which is planned with a view to the subsequent erection of a National Gallery and Museum, to complete a really noble pile of buildings. And it is well worth while to go inside. The Library is absolutely free to everybody, contains over 110,000 volumes, and has accommodation for 600 readers. An interesting feature is the large newspaper-room, where scores of working-men can be seen reading papers and magazines from all parts of the world. At the back of the same building are the painting and sculpture galleries, with which is connected a school of art and design. Behind these again is a museum. In the galleries there are a few good modern paintings, and a large number of mediocre ones. The statuary consists mainly of well-executed casts and four marble statues by the late Mr. Summers. The museum is only likely to be of interest to entomologists and mineralogists, the collection in both these departments being considered very good. The foundation and the success of the whole of this institution are almost entirely due to the late Sir Redmond Barry, who did almost as much for the University, which has also been exceedingly useful and successful from every point of view. As a building it is not equal to the Sydney University, although it possesses a splendid Gothic Hall, the gift of Sir Samuel Wilson, who now lives at Hughenden. In connection with the University is an excellent Zoological Museum, which is interesting to more than specialists.

Other fine buildings are the Government Offices, the Town Hall with its enormous organ, the Post Office, the International Exhibition--all built on a truly metropolitan scale, which is even exceeded by the palatial hugeness of the Government House, the ugliness of which is proverbial throughout Australia. But, perhaps, the class of buildings, which must in every Australian city most excite the surprise of the visitor, are the hospitals and asylums. There are no less than ten splendid structures in Melbourne devoted to charitable purposes. The Roman Catholics have built a fine cathedral, but it is not yet finished. The Church of England is collecting money for a similar purpose. Meanwhile the prettiest church belongs to the Presbyterians. None of the other churches are in any way remarkable. Anyone who has not seen the London Mint will find the Melbourne Mint worth a visit. The Observatory contains one of the largest telescopes in the world; and even if there are no races going on, the Flemington Racecourse is a 'lion' of the largest dimensions. There are four theatres, only one of which is well-fitted up. The visitor will notice that drinking bars are invariable and very disagreeable accompaniments of every theatre. One bar is generally just opposite the entrance to the dress circle, an arrangement which is particularly annoying to ladies.

Altogether, the public buildings of Melbourne do the greatest credit to the public spirit of the colonists, and offer substantial testimony to the largeness of their views and the thoroughness of their belief in the future of their country. There is certainly no city in England which can boast of nearly as many fine buildings, or as large ones, proportionately to its size, as Melbourne. And this is the more remarkable, remembering, that even in the existing hard times, masons are getting 10s. 6d. a day of eight hours, and often a very dawdling eight hours too.

The Botanic Gardens, just outside the town, are well worth a visit. They have no great scientific pretensions, as their name would imply, but are merely pleasure-grounds, decked with all the variety of flowers which this land of Cockaigne produces in abundance. Besides these, there are several pretty reserves, notably the Fitzroy, Carlton, and University Gardens, and the Regent's Park, which are all well kept and refreshing to the eye after the dust and glare of the town.

The proportions of the commercial buildings and business premises are on the same large and elaborate scale. Of the architecture, as a rule, the less said the better; but everything is at least more spacious than at home. The climate and the comparative cheapness of land give the colonists an aversion to height in their buildings, and even in the busiest parts of Melbourne most of the buildings have only two stories--i.e., a ground-floor and one above--and I can hardly think of any with more than three. The sums which banking companies pay for the erection of business premises are enormous. Thirty to sixty thousand pounds is the usual cost of their headquarters. The large insurance companies have also caught the building mania, and the joint-stock companies which are now springing up in all directions emulate them. The Australian likes to have plenty of elbow-room. He cannot understand how wealthy merchants can work in the dingy dens which serve for the offices of many a London merchant prince. In this matter, contrary to his usual practice, he is apt to consider the surface rather than what is beneath it; and it is an accepted maxim in commercial circles that money spent on buildings--which is of course borrowed in England at English rates of interest--is amongst the cheapest forms of advertising a rising business and keeping an established business going. Nobody in a young country has a long memory, and nothing is so firmly established but that it may be overthrown if it does not keep up with the times.

The general run of shops are little better than in English towns of the same size, if we except those of some dozen drapers and ironmongers in Melbourne, and two or three in Sydney, which are exceptionally good. Of these it may be said that they would be creditable to London itself. Both trades are much more comprehensive than in England. A large Melbourne draper will sell you anything, from a suit of clothes to furniture, where he comes into competition with the ironmonger, whose business includes agricultural machinery, crockery and plate. The larger firms in both these trades combine wholesale and retail business, and their shops are quite amongst the sights of Australia. Nowhere out of an exhibition and Whiteley's is it possible to meet so heterogeneous a collection. A peculiarity of Melbourne is that the shop-windows there are much better set out than is customary in England. It is not so in Sydney. Indeed Melbourne has decidedly the best set of shops, not only in outward appearance, but as to the variety and quality of the articles sold in them. Next to the drapers and ironmongers, the booksellers' shops are the most creditable. The style of the smaller shops in every colonial town is as English as English can be. The only difference is in the prices, but of that more anon when we go into the shops.

The river Yarra runs through the city, and is navigable as far as its centre by coasting steamers and all but the larger sailing craft. Above the harbour it is lined with trees and very pretty, and in spite of many windings it is wide enough for boat-races. Below it is uninteresting, and chiefly remarkable for the number and variety of the perfumes which arise from the manufactories on its banks. Next to the monotony of the Suez Canal, with which it presents many points of resemblance, I know few things more tiresome than the voyage up the Yarra in an intercolonial steamer of 600 or 700 tons, which goes aground every ten minutes, and generally, as if on purpose, just in front of a boiling-down establishment.

If the Australian cities can claim a sad eminence, if not an actual supremacy, in the number of their public houses, of which there are no less than 1,120 in Melbourne, I am sorry to say that they are as much behind London in their ideas of the comforts of an hotel as London is behind San Francisco. Melbourne is certainly better off than Sydney or Adelaide, but bad are its best hotels. Of these Menzies' and the Oriental are most to be recommended; after these try the United Club Hotel, or, if you be a bachelor, Scott's. The hotels, I think without exception, derive their chief income from the bar traffic, with which, at all but the few I have mentioned, you cannot help being brought more or less into contact. Lodgers are quite a secondary consideration. This is very disagreeable for ladies. The best hotels, moreover, have no *table d'hote*--only the old-fashioned coffee and commercial rooms; so that if you are travelling *en famille* you have no choice but to have your meals in a private sitting-room. For a bachelor, who is not particular so long as his rooms are clean, and can put up with plain fare, there need, however, be no difficulty in getting accommodation; but anyone who wishes to be comfortable had better live at the clubs, which in every one of the 'capitals' are most liberal in their hospitality, and have bedrooms on their premises. Visitors to the colony are made honorary members for a month on the introduction of any two members, and the term is extended to six months on the small subscription of a guinea a month. The Melbourne Club is the best appointed in the Colonies. The rooms are comfortable, and decently though by no means luxuriously furnished, and a very fair table is kept. The servants wear full livery. There is a small library, all the usual appurtenances of a London club, and a racquet-court. The other clubs, though less pretentious, are all comfortable.

Your colonial rarely walks a step farther than he can help, and of course laziness is well provided with cabs and omnibuses. You can take your choice between one-horse waggonettes and hansoms, though a suspicion of Bohemia still lingers about the latter. Happily Mrs. Grundy has never introduced 'growlers.' The waggonettes are light boxes on wheels, covered in with oil-cloth, which can be rolled up in a few seconds if the weather is fine or warm. It is strange that victorias like those in Paris have never been tried in this warm climate. A few years ago Irish jaunting-cars and a jolting vehicle called a 'jingle' were much used, but they have slipped out of favour of late, and are now almost obsolete. The fares are usually moderate, ranging from a shilling for a quarter of an hour to the same coin for the first mile, and sixpence for every subsequent one. Cabby is fairly civil, but, as at home, always expects more than his legal fare.

Nowhere do omnibuses drive a more thriving trade than in Melbourne, and they deserve it, for they are fast, clean, roomy, and well managed. The price of labour makes conductors too expensive a luxury, and passengers have to put their fare--in most cases threepence--into a little glass box close to the driver's seat. This unfortunate man, in addition to looking after the horses, and opening and shutting the door by means of a strap tied to his foot, which you pull when you want to get out, has to give change whenever a little bell is rung, and to see that the threepences in the glass box correspond to the number of passengers. Yet not only does he drive fast and carefully along the crowded thoroughfares, but it is difficult to escape without paying. Several times when a 'bus has been crowded I have tried the effect of omitting payment. Invariably the driver has touched his bell, and if that is not attended to, he puts his face to the chink through which change is passed, and having re-counted the number of people in the 'bus, civilly intimates that 'some gentleman has forgotten to put in his fare.' Where the omnibus companies have not penetrated, waggonettes similar to those previously described pioneer the road, and on some well-frequented lines they run in competition with the omnibuses.

I don't know that it would be true to say that the number of horses and vehicles in the streets strikes the stranger's eye as a rule. A man accustomed to the traffic of London streets passes over the traffic of Melbourne, great as it is for a town of its size, without notice. But I think he cannot but notice the novel nature of the Melbourne traffic, the prevalence of that light four-wheeled vehicle called the 'buggy,' which we have imported via America, and the extraordinary number of horsemen he meets. The horses at first sight strike the eye unpleasantly. They look rough, and are rarely properly groomed. But, as experience will soon teach the stranger, they are far less delicate than English horses. They get through a considerably greater quantity of work, and are less fatigued at the end of it.

A walk down Collins Street or Flinders Lane would astonish some of the City Croesuses. But if a visitor really wishes to form an idea of the wealth concentrated in Melbourne, he cannot do better than spend a week walking round the suburbs, and noting the thousands of large roomy houses and well-kept gardens which betoken incomes of over two thousand a year, and the tens of thousands of villas whose occupants must be spending from a thousand to fifteen hundred a year. All these suburbs are connected with the town by railway. A quarter of an hour will bring you ten miles to Brighton, and twelve minutes will take you to St. Kilda, the most fashionable watering-place. Within ten minutes by rail are the inland suburbs, Toorak, South Yarra, and Kew, all three very fashionable; Balaclava, Elsterwick, and Windsor, outgrowths of St. Kilda, also fashionable; Hawthorn, which is budding well; Richmond, adjacent to East Melbourne, and middle class; and Emerald Hill and Albert Park, with a working-class population. Adjoining the city itself are North Melbourne, Fitzroy, Carlton, Hotham, and East Melbourne, all except the last inhabited by the working-classes. Emerald Hill and Hotham have handsome town halls of their own, and the larger of these suburbs form municipalities. Nearly everybody who can lives in the suburbs, and the excellence of the railway system enables them to extend much farther away from the city than in Adelaide or Sydney. It is strange that the Australian townsman should have so thoroughly inherited the English love of living as far as possible away from the scene of his business and work during the day.

The names of the suburbs afford food for reflection. Yarra is the only native name. Sir Charles Hotham and Sir Charles Fitzroy were the governors at the time of the foundation of the municipalities which bear their names. The date of the foundation of St. Kilda is evidenced by the name of its streets-- Alma, Inkerman, Redan, Malakoff, Sebastopol, Raglan, Cardigan, and Balaclava, the last of which gave its name later on to a new suburb, which grew up at one end of it. In the city proper the principal streets are named after colonial celebrities in the early days--Flinders, Bourke, Collins, Lonsdale, Spencer, Stephen, Swanston, while King, Queen, and William Streets each tell a tale. Elizabeth Street was perhaps named after the virgin queen to whose reign the accession of the Princess Victoria called attention.

As you walk round you cannot fail to notice the sunburnt faces of the people you meet. Melbourne is said to have the prettiest girls in Australia. I am no judge. On first arrival their sallow complexions strike you most disagreeably, and it is some time before you will allow that there is a pretty girl in the country. When you get accustomed to this you will recognise that as a rule they have good figures, and that though there are no beauties, a larger number of girls have pleasant features than in England. What may be called nice looking girls abound all over Australia. In dress the Melbourne ladies are too fond of bright colours, but it can never be complained against them that they are dowdy--a fault common to their Sydney, Adelaide, and English sisters--and they certainly spend a great deal of money on their dress, every article of which costs about 50 per cent. more than at home. In every town the shop girls and factory girls--in short, all the women belonging to the industrial classes--are well dressed, and look more refined than in England. Men, on the other hand, are generally very careless about their attire, and dress untidily. The business men all wear black frock-coats and top hats. They look like city men whose clothes have been cut in the country. The working-men are dressed much more expensively than at home, and there are no threadbare clothes to be seen. Everybody has a well-to-do look There is not so much bustle as in the City, but the faces of 'all sorts and conditions of men' are more cheerful, and less careworn and anxious. You can see that bread-and-butter never enters into the cares of these people; it is only the cake which is sometimes endangered. or has not sufficient plums in it.

SYDNEY.

I suppose that nearly everyone has heard of the beauties of Sydney Harbour--'our harbour,' as the Sydneyites fondly call it. If you want a description of them read Trollope's book. He has not exaggerated an iota on this point. Sydney Harbour is one of those few sights which, like Niagara, remain photographed on the memory of whoever has been so fortunate as to see them. With this difference, however--the impression of Niagara is instantaneous; it stamps itself upon you in a moment, and though further observation may make the details more clear, it cannot add to the depth of the impressions. But Sydney Harbour grows upon you. At the first glance I think you will be a little disappointed. It is only as you drink in each fresh beauty that its wonderful loveliness takes possession of you. The more you explore its creeks and coves--forming altogether 260 miles of shore--the more familiar you become with each particular headland or reach, the greater your enchantment. You fall in love with it, so to speak, and often I look up at the water-colour sketch of Double Bay which hangs over my dining-room mantelpiece, and hope the hope which partakes of expectation, that before long I shall see Sydney Harbour again.

And it is as admirable from a practical as from an artistic point of view. The *Austral* and the *Orient* can be moored alongside natural wharves in the very heart of the city. There are coves sufficient to hold the combined fleets of the world, mercantile and naval. The outer harbour is the paradise of yachtsmen; the inner, of oarsmen. The gardens of suburban villas run down to the water's edge along the headlands and points, and there are thousands of unoccupied building sites from which you can enjoy a view fit for the gods.

One feels quite angry with the town for being so unworthy of its site. Certainly, one of the greatest charms of the harbour must have been wanting when it was uninhabited, and the view of the city and suburbs as you come up into port is as charming and picturesque, as that of Melbourne from Port Philip is commonplace and repellent. But when you get near the wharf the charm vanishes. Never was there a more complete case of distance lending enchantment to the view. Not but that there are plenty of fine buildings, public and private; but the town is still much farther back in its chrysalis stage than Melbourne. Time alone can, and is rapidly making away with the old tumble-down buildings which spoil the appearance of their neighbours. But time cannot easily widen the streets of Sydney, nor rectify their crookedness. They were originally dug out by cart-ruts, whereas those of nearly every other town in Australia were mapped out long before they were inhabited. But if they were not so ill-kept, and the footpaths so wretchedly paved, I could forgive the narrowness and crookedness of the Sydney streets, on account of their homely appearance. They are undeniably old friends, such as you can meet in hundreds of towns in Europe. Their very unsuitableness for the practical wants of a large city becomes a pleasant contrast to the practical handsomeness of Melbourne and Adelaide. The size and handsomeness of individual buildings is lost in the Sydney streets. You look at the street from one end, and put it down in your mind as no better than a lane; you walk down it without noticing the merits of the buildings it contains; whereas in Melbourne both the general effect and each individual building are shown off to the greatest advantage; but there is a certain picturesqueness and old-fashionedness about Sydney, which brings back pleasant memories of Old England, after the monotonous perfection of Melbourne and Adelaide.

The most unpleasant feature about Sydney is, that there is a thoroughly untidy look about the place. It is in a perennial state of *déshabille*; whereas Melbourne nearly always has its dress-clothes on. In keeping with the wretched pavements, the muddy crossings, and the dust, are the clothes of the people you meet in the streets. Nobody seems to care much how they dress, and without being exactly countrified in their apparel, the Sydneyites succeed in looking pre-eminently dowdy.

The water-supply is not always quite as plentiful as could be wished; but on the other hand, there is an excellent system of deep drainage, and the eye is not offended by open sewers, as in Melbourne. You will notice that there are not so many private carriages here, and fewer horsemen. The traffic appears greater, but this is entirely owing to the narrowness of the streets. It is not so rapid, as you will easily perceive.

You land, as I think I mentioned, in the heart of the city, and, unless you prefer Shanks's pony, must perforce take a hansom to your hotel, or, if you have much luggage, two hansoms, for four-wheelers are almost unknown. In compensation, the Sydney hansoms are the cleanest and fastest you will ever have the good fortune to come across. Steam trams run out to the railway station, which is at the farther end of the town, and to all the suburbs. There is practically but one hotel to go to--Petty's--and that very inferior. In most matters of this kind Sydney is only a second-rate edition of Melbourne.

The beauties of Sydney are certainly rather natural than artificial, and since one can always see a big town more or less like Melbourne, whilst the scenery of Sydney Harbour is almost unique of its kind, if I were obliged to see only one of the two places, I would rather see Sydney. But although, Sydney is poorly laid out, it must not be imagined that it is poorly built. On the contrary. Its buildings are put in the shade as regards size by those of Melbourne but if you had not seen Melbourne first, you would certainly have been surprised by the number and size of the public buildings of Sydney. The rich man loses his sense of the proportionate value of moneys. But

Sydney has the great advantage of possessing superior building material in a red and grey sandstone of great durability, which forms the substratum of the whole district in which it is built, while Melbourne has mainly to rely on a blue stone found at some distance, and has to import the stone for its best buildings from either Sydney or Tasmania. I must confess too, that I prefer the general style of architecture in Sydney to that most common in Melbourne. First and foremost, owing to the more limited area of the business part of the town, the Sydney buildings are much loftier. Melbourne and Adelaide always look to me as if some one had taken his seat upon the top of them and squashed them down. Sydney is taller and more irregular. It climbs up and down a whole series of hills, and protrudes at all kinds of unexpected points. The city proper has no very definite boundaries, and you hardly know where the city begins and the suburbs end.

Of the public buildings of Sydney, the handsomest are the Treasury, the Colonial Secretary's office, and the Lands Office, each four or five stories high, and close to the water's edge. The Colonial Secretary's office is only second to the Melbourne Law Courts amongst the completed buildings of Australia. It is lofty, massive, and dignified outwardly, elegant and spacious inside, although it has been fitted up in the most incongruous fashion with odds and ends of third-rate statuary, imitation bronzes, etc., until it looks like an old curiosity-shop. The University, though comparatively an old building, still holds its ground amongst the best, and may well be proud of its splendidly proportioned hall, built in fifteenth-century Gothic. The Roman Catholic Cathedral, which has just been opened, is also well proportioned. The length is 350 feet; width within transept 118 feet; width of nave and aisle 74 feet; height about ninety feet. There is to be a central tower 120 feet high, and two towers with spires which will rise to a height of 260 feet. The Anglican Cathedral, though not large, is a handsome building with two towers, in fourteenth-century Gothic. The Post Office will for many years remain a fragment of what may or may not be a handsome building. The Town Hall has evidently been built with the idea of at all hazards making it larger than the Melbourne Town Hall. So far it is a success. But architecturally it is nothing more than a splendid failure--over-decorated and ginger-bready. Curiously enough it is built upon the site of the burial-place of the early settlement---forming a sort of Westminster Abbey for the first settlers. There are four theatres, but none well fitted or decorated. Palatial hospitals and asylums of course abound, but the Parliament House is wretchedly small.

Unfortunately Sydney has very few reserves, and those few she keeps in bad order, with the exception of the Botanical Garden, situated on an arm of the land almost entirely surrounded by water. It is the most charming public garden I have ever seen; inferior to that of Adelaide in detail, but superior in the *tout ensemble*. Almost equally beautiful is the situation of Government House, a comfortable Tudor mansion, but rather small for purposes of entertainment.

Amongst the commercial buildings, the new head offices of the Australian Mutual Provident Society are pre-eminent. They cost no less than £50,000. The banks are not equal to either the Melbourne or the Adelaide banks. But the insurance offices, warehouses, etc., though not nearly as numerous, are quite up to the Melbourne standard in size, although for the reasons already given they do not show to so great an advantage as their merit deserves. Of the appearance of the shops I have already written in my letter about Melbourne. They are not so fine as in Melbourne nor so well stocked, and are pretty much on a level with those in an English town of the same size.

The names of the principal streets proclaim the age of the town. George Street and Pitt Street are the two main thoroughfares, and there are Castlereagh, Liverpool, and William Streets, while King, Hunter, Bligh, Macquarie, and Philip Streets, and Darlinghurst preserve the names of the first governors. The suburbs first formed preserve the sweet-sounding native names--Wooloomooloo, Woolahra, Coogee, Bondi. Of a later date are Randwick, Newtown, Stanmore, Ashfield, Burwood, and Petersham--the last four along the railway line.

The good people of Sydney do not spend their money so much upon outward show as the Victorians. Hence the number of large houses in the suburbs is very much smaller. But whereas the country around Melbourne for miles is mostly flat as a pancake, the suburbs of Sydney literally revel in beautiful building sites. For choice, there are the water frontages below the town or up the Parramatta river, which is lined with pretty houses, whose inhabitants come up to Sydney every morning in small river steamers. The principal suburbs, however, are much closer to the city than in Melbourne, being connected by steam tramways instead of railways. New suburbs are also springing up along the railway lines, but until the railway station is brought into the centre of the town, they can never be nearly so populous as the Melbourne suburbs.

ADELAIDE.

I began with a comparison between Melbourne and Sydney, towns of 280,000 and 220,000 inhabitants respectively. The capital of South Australia, Adelaide, with its 70,000, stands, of course, upon an entirely different level; but it possesses, to an even greater degree than Sydney, all the peculiar characteristics of a capital city. If any comparison can be made between Adelaide and its sister capitals, it is with Melbourne rather than with Sydney. Adelaide is a thoroughly modern town, with all the merits and all the defects attaching to novelty. It does not possess the spirit of enterprise to so adventurous a degree as Melbourne, but neither does it approach to the languor of Sydney. In this respect it has discovered a very happy middle course. There is certainly something very provincial about the attitude of the town towards the rest of the world, but this helps to make it the more distinctive, and conduces largely to its progress. It 'goes without saying' that there cannot be the same number of large buildings as in the larger cities, that their proportions cannot be so large, that there cannot be the same facilities for business or for pleasure. But the emulation produced by the achievements of its big neighbours has resulted in making Adelaide a far more advanced town for its size than either of them. Proportionately to population, everything in Adelaide ought theoretically to be on a fourth scale of its like in Melbourne. As a matter of fact, most things are on more than half-scale, many on a two-thirds, and a few things, such as the Botanic Garden, the Exchange, the Banks of South Australia and Adelaide, are unsurpassed.

For its size, I consider Adelaide the beet-built town I know, and certainly it is the best laid out and one of the prettiest and most conveniently situated. It nestles, so to speak, at the foot of a range of high hills on a plain, which extends seven miles in length to the seashore. The approach by rail from either Port Adelaide or Glenelg is uninteresting, but directly you get out at the station the first impression is pleasing. The streets are broad and laid out in rectangular blocks as in Melbourne, and the white stone used for most of the buildings makes the town look particularly bright and lively, showing off the bustle and traffic to advantage. In the background are the hills, while on one side is the suburb of North Adelaide, on an incline divided from the city by a broad sheet of artificial water, running in the bed of the river Torrens through a half-mile deep belt of 'park-lands,' which encircle the square mile forming the city proper, and separate it from the suburbs.

The conception of this belt of verdure, on which none but public buildings may be erected, dividing the working part of the town from the residential part, has always seemed to me a masterpiece of wisdom in city planning, and hardly less admirable are the five open reserves inside the city which serve as its lungs. Ultimately the city proper will probably be almost entirely reserved for business purposes. Already very few people live within the belts who can help it, although high prices are given for sites for residences on each of the four terraces fronting the belts. Except that Adelaide is perfectly flat, while Melbourne is built on two sides of a valley, Adelaide may not inaptly be described in the words of a visitor who was returning to England by the Peninsular and Oriental route, as 'a smaller but better Melbourne.' The style of architecture is not quite so florid, but the extreme squatness of the buildings is far more noticeable here. It is no merely that the buildings are actually lower, but the look lower from being built on the flat.

Of the public buildings, the finest is the Post Office, which, though it wants an extra story to make it dignified, is, in my opinion, preferable to either the Melbourne or Sydney Post Offices. The new Institute, the Anglican Cathedral, which is lofty, the Town Hall, the Supreme Court, the Banks of South Australia, of Adelaide, and the English and Scottish Bank, and the new vice-regal residence on the hills, are all fine buildings, which would attract favourable notice in Melbourne or Sydney. Nominally there are three theatres, practically only one, but that is undoubtedly the prettiest and best in Australia. But the pride of Adelaide is its Botanic Garden, which, though unpromisingly situated on a perfectly level spot, with no water at hand, has been transformed, by means of artificial water and artificial hillocks, into the prettiest garden in the world The area is only forty acres, but every inch has been turned to the utmost advantage, and this is really a garden, while the Sydney Gardens--mark the plural--are more park-like, and those of Melbourne can hardly be called gardens, in the strict sense of the word.

The drainage is defective, but the water-supply good. There is still a great deal to be done to the footpaths, and until quite recently the municipal arrangements were in every respect almost as bad as those of Sydney. But an able, energetic, and liberal mayor, Mr. E. T. Smith, in the course of two years so stirred up the citizens that pavements have been laid down, additional gas-lights provided, the Torrens artificial lake constructed, the squares and park-lands transformed from untidy wildernesses into handsome oases, and the general aspect of the city entirely transformed. I do not know that I ever saw so much done entirely at the initiative and by the energy and persistence of a single man.

Of the shops there is not much to be said. They are not at all up to the average of most of the institutions of the town, with the one exception of those of the jewellers and silversmiths, the work in which is original and artistic, throwing altogether into the shade similar shops in Melbourne and Sydney. The cabs are all waggonettes, similar to those used in Melbourne, but drawn by two horses instead of one. Adelaide abhors hansoms. They exist, but are never used by respectable people, who have come to look upon them as unholy in themselves. The tramway system is the most complete in Australia. All the trams are drawn by horses; to such of the suburbs as are too thinly populated to have trams large waggonettes for the most part run in lieu of omnibuses. Adelaide is the only Australian town in which the American system of buying land, and making a railway to bring population to it, has been carried out. The idea was first tried with tramways, the writer having taken some part in originating and promoting it. Of the hotels of Adelaide, the best is the York. It is better than the best, in Sydney, but inferior to the best two in Melbourne.

Owing to the excellent plan on which the city is laid out, it is surrounded on every side by suburbs at the short distance of half a mile, connected by horse-tramways. Beyond these, however, there is the flourishing watering-place of Glenelg at a distance of only seven miles by train; and now that the railway has been carried into the hills, it will not be long before large suburbs grow up in them. Wealth in South Australia is more equally divided than in the sister Colonies. Hence there are only a few large mansions, but comfortable six to ten-roomed cottages abound.

HOUSES.

The inevitable 'newness' of everything cannot but strike the eye disagreeably. This is especially noticeable in the buildings and houses, few of which date back more than ten years. In the growth of towns, as well as in the progress of individuals and institutions, there are three periods to be gone through. Here the first stage is that of the log-hut. This is succeeded by the weather-board cottage, which in turn gives place to brick and stucco. Finally comes the stone building with its two or three stories. The log-hut stage is of course far past. The weather-board cottage still lingers in the poorer outskirts of Melbourne, but is extinct in Adelaide, and fast becoming extinct in Melbourne. The choice now is between brick and stone. In Sydney the abundance of stone on the spot, gives it the preference; Adelaide, with less stone, builds chiefly in brick; Melbourne, which has to get its stone from a distance, uses hardly anything else but brick. This, of course, for private houses. There are plenty of admirable stone buildings in Melbourne, as I have already mentioned.

Now that the brick and stone age is firmly established the style of your house becomes a mere matter of pounds, shillings, and pence. With wages at from nine to twelve shillings a day, and with money so much dearer than at home, the Australian has necessarily to pay a much higher rent for his house. Excluding, of course, ground-rents, which make London houses so expensive, I think one may fairly say that rents here are about double the rate they are at home, and yet, *except for the rise in the value of land* in the cities and their suburbs, house-property is by no means a remunerative investment. Nevertheless, there is always a great demand for it. The colonist is very fond of living in his own house and on his own bit of ground, and building societies and the extensive mortgage system which prevails enable him easily to gratify this desire. I believe that at least ninety out of every hundred house-properties in Australia are mortgaged up to at least two-thirds of their value. Out in the suburbs ground-rents are still low--very low indeed in comparison with the selling value. The reason of this is, that it pays to buy a house with a large piece of land attached, and to cut the land up and sell it in building allotments a few years afterwards. If you can get a fair rent for the house, the land will pay its own way.

Architecturally speaking, there is little to admire. If the public buildings fail in this respect, the private houses have at least the advantage over them, that for the most part they do not pretend to any architecture at all. Many of the architects are self-taught, and have served little or no apprenticeship to the profession. Indeed, it should rather be called a trade, since they often are merely successful builders, who have taken to planning and superintending the erection of buildings, instead of erecting them themselves. This is one reason why private houses incline rather to the practical than to the beautiful. Another cause is the practical spirit of the colonists, which looks upon expenditure for mere ornamental purposes as wasteful and extravagant. Unless a man is really rich, he cannot afford the imputation of extravagance which any architectural expenditure will bring upon him. With his business premises it is different. Everyone understands that a merchant spends money in ornamenting his business premises, just as a tradesman dresses his shop-window. But the tradesman does not dress the drawing-room window of his private house. Neither, therefore, the merchant. Besides this, it cannot be too thoroughly understood that Australia is before everything a money-making place, and that anything like unremunerative expenditure with no possible chance of profit is considered foolish in all but a man who has made his fortune. With money so dear, and the chances of turning it over rapidly so frequent and so remunerative, such expenditure becomes little less than a sin. Everything ornamental not only costs twice as dear in actual money, but the money itself is worth at least twice as much as in England.

Really large houses of the size of the manor-houses and halls which are scattered over England in tens of thousands, can be counted in Australia in scores. Of these but few have any architectural pretensions. Houses of this class cannot be built under £10,000 here, whereas in England they would cost from £4,000 to £5,000 and can be bought still cheaper. If there is any style which colonists particularly affect, it is the castellar. Both in the large houses I have just been speaking of, and in the ordinary wealthy man's house which has cost him from £3,000 to £5,000, turrets and flagstaffs abound. The passion for flagstaffs must, I think, be derived from the fact that most of the people who build these houses have had a long sea-journey from England, and retain a little ozone in their composition. There is also something assertive about a flag. A man who has a flag floating on his house is almost sure to have some character about him. Not unfrequently, when the builder of a house intends to live in it himself, he wishes to imitate his old home in England, or if he has risen in the world, some particular house of the village or town he was brought up in, which he admired in his boyhood. The man who builds for himself at least takes care to build soundly, and to have his rooms large and lofty.

By far the majority of houses are built by speculators; which means that they are very badly built, run up in a tremendous hurry, constructed of the cheapest and nastiest materials, with thin walls--in short, built for show, and not for use. Everything looks very nice in them when you walk round just after they are built, and it is only after you have lived in them eighteen months that you begin to understand why the owner was in such a hurry to sell, and would not hear of letting the house to you, even at a good rent. You know something of this in London, but not nearly to the same extent as here. In these speculative houses there is often some little attempt at ornamentation--a bow-window thrown out, or the veranda lifted to form a Gothic porch, or the drawing-room brought out beyond the rest of the house, so as to form what is known as a T cottage, though it should rather be a P, with a protrusion of the drawing-room representing the straight line, and the body of the house the loop of the P.

But the favourite type of Australian house is laid, out in an oblong block bisected by a three to eight foot passage. The first door on one side as you go in is the drawing-room, on the other the dining-room. Then follow the bedrooms, etc., with the kitchen and scullery at the end of the passage, or sometimes in a lean-to at right angles to the hinder part of the house proper. This kind of cottage is almost universal in Adelaide amongst the middle and upper middle classes, and invariable in the working-class throughout Australia. In the other colonies the upper middle classes often live in two-storied houses; i.e., ground-floor and one floor above. Their construction is almost as simple as the cottage, the only difference being that the bedrooms are on the upper story, and that a pair of narrow stairs face the front-door and take up half the passage-way, directly you get past the drawing and dining-room doom doors. The cottage is not high enough to strike the eye, but the squareness, or more properly the cubeness, of these two-storied houses is appalling. They look for all the world like houses built of cards, except that the cards are uncommonly solid. For my own part, I should never care to live in a two-storied house again, after experiencing the comfort of never having to go upstairs, and having all the rooms on the same floor. At first one is prejudiced against it. I was so, until during my second year in Australia I had to live on the third floor in Sydney. It was only then that I realized the advantages of the simpler plan.

The strong light and heat of the sun has the effect of a window-tax in limiting the size and number of the windows. A few French windows are to be found in Adelaide, but the old sashes are almost universal. Of, late a fashion has sprung up for bow-windows, which, however pretty, have here the great disadvantage of attracting the sun unpleasantly. Shutters are not much used. Venetian blinds are more common. On a hot summer day it is absolutely necessary to shut all windows and draw down the blinds if you wish to keep at all cool. About five o'clock, if there is no hot wind, the house may be opened out.

Nearly every house that can afford the space has a veranda, which sometimes stretches the whole way round. The rooms are usually lofty for their size, in winter horribly cold and draughty, in summer unbearably stuffy in small houses, the science of ventilation being of recent introduction. Even in large establishments all the living-rooms are almost always on the ground-floor, both on account of the fatigue of going up and down stairs, and owing to the paucity of servants. As a rule, the kitchens are terribly small, and in summer filled with flies. How the poor servants manage to exist in them is more than I can understand. It is no wonder they ask such high wages. In a few larger houses a merciful fashion has been adopted of making the kitchen a mere cooking galley, the cook preparing the dishes and doing all that does not require the presence of fire in a large back-kitchen. Happily every house has a bath-room, though it is often only a mere shed of wood or galvanized iron put up in the back-yard. In many of the poorer households this shed does double duty as bath-house and wash-house, or the wash-house consists of a couple of boards, with a post to keep them up, and a piece of netting overhead to keep the sun off. In larger houses, both bath-rooms and wash-houses are much the same as in England. Nearly all families do their washing, and often their ironing also, at home. Of the sanitary arrangements, it is almost impossible to speak too strongly; they are almost invariably objectionable and disgusting.

There are very few establishments large enough to indulge in the luxury of a servants'-hall, and sculleries and pantries are much smaller than in England. Even the ordinary entrance-hall of an English house has to shrink into a mere enlargement of the passage. All over the house, in fact, the accommodation is on a much more limited scale, unless it be with regard to stables, which, owing to the low price of horses, are more numerous, if less luxuriously appointed.

If the upper and middle classes suffer from want of room in their houses, and are wont to huddle much more than people in the same position would at home, the working-man is not much better off, although his four or five-roomed cottage at twelve shillings to fifteen shillings a week is more easily within his means than the five shillings a week that he paid in England. I do not of course mean that the working-man here knows anything of model cottages, such as are seen on large estates in England. I should even say that during the first year or two after his arrival there is little improvement in his habitation; but before long he acquires a small freehold, and with the aid of a building society becomes his own landlord. Directly he has reached this stage, an improvement is visible in his condition. It is difficult to over-estimate the social value of the work that has been done by building societies. In the suburbs of the large towns you see whole townships built entirely by these societies; every inhabitant of these townships in the course of a few years becomes a proprietor, and the society further aids him by making loans to him on mortgage of his property. It is the defect of these townships that the houses are all as like one another as peas in a pod--four-roomed squares or six-roomed oblongs built of red brick, and with every detail exactly the same; but their plainness and similarity does not detract from their manifest virtues.

Terraces and attached houses are universally disliked, and almost every class of suburban house is detached and stands in its own garden. These gardens are laid out much in the English fashion; but there is little need of greenhouses, and unless you have water laid on to your lawn, it is difficult to keep it green in summer. In Adelaide but few people try to keep lawns; the summer sun is too scorching, and towards February and March the gardens look dreadfully dried up. But on the other hand, flowers of all kinds grow in abundance, and to a size which they rarely attain in colder climates. The garden needs little attention beyond the summer watering and you can get flowers all the year round. Fruit-trees grow with wonderful rapidity and bear most abundantly.

With the aid of the hills you get several climates within a small area, and in Adelaide especially the abundance of flowers and fruit is all that can be desired. There is naturally some tendency to coarseness, especially in the fruit. The price of labour makes it difficult to keep large gardens in good order. For this reason few people keep large gardens. Another thing that accounts for the smallness of the gardens attached to middle and working-class houses, which are often no more than patches, is the speculation in land. The smaller the portions into which the speculator cuts up his building sections, the more he gets for them. I myself on one occasion bought an eight-acre section of land in one block for £1,100, cut it up into blocks of an eighth of an acre each, and resold it within six weeks for a little over £2,000. This land-speculation is quite a feature of Australian life, and at certain periods it is difficult to lose money by it. Large gardens are generally long leaseholds or freeholds belonging to rich people, who will not sell during their lifetime. At their death their gardens are cut up into small blocks and yield large profits. Nor do I think that the love of gardening is at all common here; it is not a sufficiently exciting occupation.

FURNITURE.

I closed my last letter with an account of the way in which houses are built here. I am now going to try to describe their contents. And perhaps the best way to do this will be to describe a type of each class of house, omitting all exceptions, which are necessarily numerous where so large a field has to be covered.

We will begin at the top of the tree. Whilst the ambition of the wealthy colonist not unfrequently finds vent in building a large house, he has generally been brought up in too rough a school to care to furnish it even decently. His notion of furniture begins and ends with upholstery, and I doubt whether he ever comes to look upon this as more than things to sit on, stand on, lie on, eat off and drink off The idea of deriving any pleasure from the beauty of his surroundings rarely enters into his head, and it is not uncommon to find a man who is making £5,000 a year amply satisfied with what an Englishman with one-tenth of his income would deem the barest necessaries. The Australian Croesus is generally very little of a snob, though often his 'lady' has a taste for display. When this desire for grandeur has led them to furnish expensively, they are unable to furnish prettily, and usually feel much less comfortable in their drawing-room, in which they never set foot except when there is company--than when their chairs and tables were made by a working carpenter or with their own hands out of a few deal boards.

One or two millionaires have had upholsterers out from Gillow's and Jackson and Graham's to furnish their houses in the latest and most correct fashion, and many colonists who go on a trip to England bring back with them drawing and dining room suites; but even then there is an entire want of individuality about the Australian's house--which is the more remarkable seeing how much his individuality has been brought out by his career, and shows itself in his general actions and opinions. He may know how to dogmatize on theology and politics, but when he gets down to furniture he confesses that his eye is out of focus. The furniture imported or (in Melbourne) made by the large upholsterers is, with few exceptions, more gorgeous than pretty; whence one may reasonably infer that the taste of their customers--when they have any--is better suited by the grandiose than the artistic. But most of the expensively furnished houses show plainly that the upholsterer has been given *carte blanche* to do what he will. Look at his shop-window, and you may make a shrewd guess at his customer's drawing-room.

Nor is the furniture universal in Australia, as one would naturally suppose, after the style of that in Italy and the South of France. The frowsy carpets and heavy solid chairs of England's cold and foggy climate reign supreme beneath the Austral sun. The Exhibitions have done something towards reforming our domestic interiors, but it will be a long time before the renaissance of art as applied to households, which appears to be taking place in England, makes its way here in any considerable force.

But instead of generalizing, it is time we should go through Muttonwool's house room by room. On entering the drawing-room the first thing that strikes the eye is the carpet, with a stiff set pattern large enough to knock you down, and of a rich gaudy colour. You raise your eyes--find opposite them the regulation white marble mantelpiece, more or less carved, and a gilt mirror, which we will hope is not protected from the flies by green netting. Having made a grimace, you sit down upon one of the chairs. There are nine in the room besides the sofa--perhaps an ottoman--and you can take your choice between the 'gent's' armchair, the lady's low-chair, and the six high ones. If they are not in their night-shirts you can examine the covering-- usually satin or perhaps cretonne. The pattern is unique, being, I should think, specially manufactured for the colonial market. Bright hues prevail. Occasional chairs have only lately been introduced, and the whole suite is in unison, though harmony with the carpet has been overlooked, or rather never thought of, the two things having been chosen separately, and without any idea that it would be an improvement if they were to match.

As for the make of the chairs, they are to be found in plenty of English middle-class drawing-rooms even now. The shape may be named the 'deformed.' The back is carved out into various contortions of a horse-shoe, with a bar across the middle which just catches you in the small of the back, and is a continual reproach if you venture to lean against it. The wood of which the chairs are made is mahogany, walnut, or cedar. The large round or oval table which stands in the middle of the room is of the same wood, and so are the card-table, the Davenport, the chiffonier, and that Jacob's-ladder-like what-not in the corner. In some houses the upholsterer has stuffed the room with useless tables. Of course there is a fender and fire-irons, and probably a black doleful-looking grate, which during two-thirds of the year is stuffed with paper shavings of all the colours of the rainbow and several others which good Mother Nature forgot to put into it. On the chimney-piece is a Louis XVI. clock and a pair of ornaments to match. A piano, tune immaterial, is a *sine quâ non* even in a middle-class house, but when Muttonwool has got all these things--in short, paid his upholsterer's bill--he thinks a ten-pound note should cover the rest of his drawing-room furniture. Household gods are terribly deficient, and it would not be difficult to fancy yourself in a lodging-house. There may be a few odds and ends picked up on the overland route, and a set of stereotyped ornaments bought at an auction sale or sent out as 'sundries' in a general cargo; but of *bric-à-brac*, in the usual acceptation of the term, there is little or none.

As for the pictures, they are altogether abominable. Can you imagine a man with £5,000 a year (or £500, for that matter) covering his walls with chromos? The inferior kinds of these 'popularizers of art,' as the papers call them, have an immense sale here. Even when a wealthy man has been told that it is his duty to buy pictures, the chances are that he will attend an auction and pick up rubbish at low prices, rubbing his hands over what he considers a good bargain; or if he wants to tell his visitors how much he gave for his pictures he gets mediocre work with a name on it. A recent number of the *Adelaide Punch* has a caricature entitled "Igh Art in Adelaide,' which though of course a caricature, is worth quoting as showing how the wind blows: 'Tallowfat, pointing to a picture in a dealer's shop, *loq*.: "What's the price of that there thing with the trees and the 'ut in the distance?" Dealer: "That, sir! that's a gem by Johnstone" (a local artist of some merit)--"twenty guineas, sir." Tallowfat: "Twenty tomfools!" "What d'ye take me for? Why, I bought a picture twice that size, with much more colour in it, and a frame half as thick again, and I only paid ten for it! Show us something with more style."' A few men have good pictures, but I hardly know anyone who has any good engravings. Muttonwool can see no difference between a proof before letters and the illustrations from the newspapers, which may be seen pasted on the walls of every small shop and working-man's cottage. That there is a taste for pictures here is undeniable. But that is common to every child till it knows how to read, and will want a deal of educating before it can be called 'art.'

We will now go into the dining-room, which is probably the best furnished room in the house. It is not easy to make a dining-room look out of joint provided you are not particular about the cost, though there is a very wide margin between the decent and the handsome. The upholstery is much the same as in an ordinary upper middle-class house in England--sofa, sideboard, chiffonier, two easy and eight or ten upright chairs in cedar frames and covered with leather, marble mantelpiece and clock, Louis XVI. glass, and a carpet which is at any rate better than the drawing-room one. If there is a breakfast-room it is a smaller edition of the dining-room. The study is chiefly remarkable for the absence of books, or for an inappropriateness to the owner's tastes which smacks of a job-lot. The bedrooms are disappointing. Pictures and knick-knacks rarely extend beyond the 'company' precincts. Muttonwool would think it a waste of good bawbees to put pretty things in the bedrooms, where no one but the family will see them. In these rooms he is *au naturel*, and with all his good-nature and genuineness he is rather a rough fellow. The brute is expelled from the drawing-room, but he jumps in again at the bedroom window. As for the servants' rooms, anything is good enough for them. Probably the master himself was contented with still less in his younger days. The kitchen is ordinarily very poorly provided with utensils. Ranges and stoves are only found in the wealthier houses, the usual cooking apparatus being a colonial oven--a sort of box with fire above and below, which is very convenient for burning wood, the usual fuel throughout Australia.

I think this is about as much as need be said about an average wealthy Australian's house; but before going on to describe middle-class homes, I must ask you to remember that all large colonial houses are not furnished on this wise. There are a large number of people in Australia, and especially in Victoria, who have as good an idea of how to furnish as other middle-class Englishmen--though perhaps that is not saying much. But in articles of this kind I am obliged to strike an average. The type of house I have described is the most common. You must leave a marain on either side of it according to the education and tastes of the owner. And here let me note that in Melbourne houses are certainly more expensively, and perhaps better furnished than in any of the other towns. The Victorians have a much greater love of show than any of their fellow-Australians. Where a Sydney man spends £400 on his furniture you may safely predict that a Melbourner will spend £600. Consequently the furniture establishments in the latter city are much superior to those in the former, and that although, owing to the enormous duty-25 per cent.--but little English furniture is imported into Victoria.

Let us now hie us to humbler abodes, and visit an eight-roomed cottage, inhabited by a young solicitor whose income is from £500 to £1000 a year. Here the whole drawing-room suite is in cretonne or rep, and comprises the couch, six chairs, and lady's and gent's easy-chairs, which we saw before at Muttonwool's. The carpet is also ditto. The glass, ornaments, etc., are similar, but on a smaller scale; and if there are any pictures on the wall they are almost bound to be chromos, for whilst Croesus sometimes invests in expensive paintings, the middle-class, who cannot afford to give from £100 upwards for a picture, will make no effort to obtain something moderately good, such as can be easily obtained in England for a very small outlay. The gasalier is bronze instead of glass. The real living-room of the house is the dining-room, which is therefore the best furnished, and on a tapestry carpet are a leather couch, six balloon-back carved chairs, two easy-chairs, a chiffonier, a side-table, and a cheap chimney-glass. In the best bedroom the bedstead is a tubular half-tester, the toilet-ware gold and white, the carpet again tapestry. Throughout the house the furniture is made of cedar. The kitchen is summarily disposed of; Biddy has to content herself with d table, dresser, safe, pasteboard and rolling-pin, and a couple of chairs. Her bedroom furniture is even more scanty--a paillasse on trestles, a chair, a half-crown looking-glass, an old jug and a basin on a wooden table. Even in the houses of the wealthy poor Biddy is very badly treated in this respect. In Muttonwool's house, if he keeps two servants, they both sleep in one room, and not improbably share the same basin. Servants are undoubtedly troublesome to a degree in Australia, but it is not altogether a satisfactory feature in colonial life that the provision made for their comfort is literally nil.

Having seen the £600 a year cottage it is almost needless to visit the £300 and £400, belonging to clerks and the smaller shopkeepers. The style is the same, but the quantity and quality inferior. For instance, the drawing-room carpet is tapestry instead of Brussels; the dining-room furniture is covered with horse-hair instead of leather, and so on. We will go into the next cottage--less pretentious-looking and a little smaller. The rent is twelve shillings a week, and it belongs to a carpenter in good employ. Here there is no drawing-room, but the parlour aspires to comfort quite undreamt of by an English tradesman. Our old friends the horse-hair cedar couch, the gent's and lady's chairs together with four balloon high chairs, turn up again. There is a four-foot chiffonier, a tapestry carpet, a gilt chimney-glass, a hearthrug, a bronze fender and fire-irons, and a round table with turned pillar and carved claws. In the parents' bedroom are a half-tester bedstead with coir-fibre or woollen flock mattress, two cane chairs, washstand, toilet-table, glass and ware, towel-horse, chest of drawers, and a couple of yards of bedside carpet. The two youngest children sleep in this room, and three or four others in the second bedroom, where the bedsteads are less showy and the ware very inferior. The carpet is replaced by china matting. The chest of drawers does duty as a toilet-table, and there are of course no such luxuries as towel-horses. Yet, take it all in all, Chips has much to be thankful for.

With labour so dear as it is here, it is wonderful to think that a working-man can furnish, and furnish comfortably, a four-roomed cottage for £27; and yet this is what has recently been done in Melbourne by my friend Hornyhand, who is a common labourer, earning only eight to nine shillings a day, and paying about as much a week for rent. He is really uncommonly well off, everything in his house being brand-new; and yet, as he tells me, he is absolutely at the root of the honest social tree--the worst paid of the working-classes. I think it worth while to subjoin his bill. He certainly has not gone in for luxuries, but then he is of a frugal mind. If he wanted it, his house could be as well furnished as Chips'; but he doesn't see any object in wasting money on that kind of thing, and is content with little:

Parlour.   £ s. d.

Cedar polished couch, covered with horse-hair	2 10 0
Four cane-seat chairs, each 7s. 6d.	1 10 0
Cedar polished table, 3 ft. 6 in., on claws	1 10 0

Maple rocking-chair, with elbows	0	17	6
Carpet	1	5	0
Hearthrug, 8s. 6d. fender, 9s. irons, 6s. 6d.	1	4	0

Bedroom.

French bedstead, 4 ft. 6 in. by 6 ft. 6 in.	1	15	0
Pair paillasses		12	6
Woollen flock mattrass	1	0	0
Woollen flock bolster and 2 pillows		8	0
Washstand, and rail attached		10	6
Toilet table, to match		10	6
Toilet glass, 14 in. by 10 in.		8	6
2 cane-scat chairs (Albert), 6s. each		12	0
4 yards matting at 9d.		3	0
Toilet-ware, six pieces		12	6

Second Bedroom.

2 French bedsteads, 3 ft. by 6 ft. 6 in. at 30s.	3	0	0
4 paillasses, at 10s. per pair	1	0	0
2 woollen flock mattrasses, at 16. 3d. each	1	12	6
2 bolsters, flock, at 4s. 6d. each		9	0
2 pillows, flock, at 3s. each		6	0
Toilet chest of drawers (to serve for toilet table), cedar	2	5	0
Toilet glass, 14 in. by 10 in.		7	0
Washstand, 2 ft. 6 in.		12	0
Wash, etc., 6 pieces		12	6

Kitchen.

Deal table, turned legs, varnished	10 6
2 wood chairs, each 4s. 6d.	9 0
Safe in Kauri pine	10 6
Pasteboard and rolling-pin	4 0
	£27 7 0

Note.--That if he had not had two children to provide for in a second bedroom, nor indulged in the luxury of a chest of drawers, the whole of his furnishing would only have cost him £17 3s.

Before closing this letter, a word as to what may be called the accessories of the household. But few families have any large quantity of plate, and electro has almost entirely superseded silver; metal is not common for dishes, and is quite unknown for plates. Nor is the crockery at all a strong point even in the wealthiest houses. In the shops it is almost impossible to get anything satisfactory in this line; and until the exhibitions, nine Australians out of ten had no idea what was meant by hand-painted china. The difference between china and earthenware is, it goes almost without saying, little if at all appreciated, much less that between hand-painted and stamped ware. The display of cut-glass at the exhibitions was almost as great a revelation to colonists as that of porcelain; hitherto all middle-class and most wealthy households have been contented with the commonest stuff. Table-cloths and napkins are also very second-rate, and sheets are almost invariably of calico.

SERVANTS.

That servants are the plague of life seems to be an accepted axiom amongst English ladies of the upper middle class. When I hear them discussing their grievances over their afternoon tea, I wish them no worse fate than to have the management of an Australian household for a week. It is not every Englishwoman whose peace of mind would survive the trial. Many a young English wife have I seen unhappy in her married life in the colonies, mainly on account of her domestics. And yet I doubt whether the colonial mistress makes as much fuss about her real wrongs as the English one about her imaginary grievances. Of course she can, if drawn out, tell you enough ridiculous stories about her servants to fill a number of *Punch*; but if they are only fools she is well content, and it is only when she is left servantless for two or three days that she waxes wroth.

Where mistresses are many and servants are few, it goes almost without saying that large establishments are out of the question. Given equal incomes, and the English mistress has twice as many servants as the Australian, and what is more, twice as competent ones. Even our friend Muttonwool only has six coachman, boy, cook, housemaid, nurse, and parlourmaid. I don't suppose there are a hundred households in all Australia which keep a butler pure and simple, though there must be several thousand with what is generically known as a man-servant, who gets twenty-five shillings a week, all found. A coachman's wages are on the average about the same. The 'boy' gets ten shillings. Man-cooks are rare. A decent female cook, who ranks out here as first-class, earns from fifteen shillings to a pound a week. For this sum she is supposed to know something about cooking; yet I have known one in receipt of a weekly guinea look with astonishment at a hare which had been sent to her master as a present, and declare that it was 'impossible to make soup out of that thing.' After a little persuasion she was induced to try to make hare-soup after Mrs. Beeton's recipe, but the result was such as to try the politeness of her master's visitors. This lack of decent cooks is principally due to the lack of establishments large enough to keep kitchenmaids. Would-be cooks have no opportunity of acquiring their art by training from their superiors; they gain their knowledge by experiments on their employers' digestions; never staying long in one place, they learn to make some new dishes at each house they go to, and gradually rise in the wages-scale.

Directly you come to incomes below a thousand a year, the number of servants is often reduced to a maid-of-all-work, more or less competent according to her wages, which run from seven to fifteen shillings a week. At the former price she knows absolutely nothing; at the latter something of everything. She cooks, washes, sweeps, dusts, makes the beds, clears the baths, and answers the, door. All is grist that comes to her mill; and if she is Jill-of-all-trades and mistress of none, one must admit that an English-bred servant would not be one quarter so suitable to colonial requirements. Of course she is independent, often even cheeky, but a mistress learns to put up with occasional tantrums, provided the general behaviour and character are good. When we were first out here we used to run a-muck with our servants about once a week; but now we find it better to bear the ills we have than fly to others which we know not of. Our present Lizzie is impertinent to a degree when reproved; but then she can cook decently, and she is the first decent cook we have had since we have been out here. When you have lived on colonial fare for a few months, a good plain dinner covers a multitude of sins.

Unfortunately, four-fifths of our servants are Irish--liars and dirty. These Irish are less impertinent than the colonials; but if you do get hold of a well trained colonial, she is worth her weight in gold on account of her heterogeneity. Your Irish immigrant at eight and ten shillings a week has as often as not never been inside any other household than her native hovel, and stares in astonishment to find that you don't keep a pig on your drawing-room sofa. On entering your house, she gapes in awe of what she considers the grandeur around her, and the whole of her first day's work consists of ejaculating 'Lor' and 'Goodness!' We once had a hopeful of this kind who, after she had been given full instructions as to how a rice-pudding was to be made, sat down and wept bitterly for half an hour, till--her mistress having told her to 'bake'--the happy thought struck her to put a dish full of rice in the oven, *sans* milk *sans* eggs, *sans* everything. Another Biddy, engaged by a friend of ours, having to make a yeast-cake, put it under her bed-clothes 'just to plump it a bit.' A third, having been given a bill-of-fare for the day, put soup, meat, and pudding all into one pot, and served them up *au pot-pourri*.

But if Biddy is trying to the patience, her stupidity is to a mistress accustomed to English ways almost more bearable than the 'go-as-you-please'--if I may borrow a phrase from the new American athletic contests--of the colonial young lady, who comes to be engaged in the most elegant of dresses, bows as she enters the room, seats herself, and smilingly remarks, that she has heard that Mrs. So-and-So is wanting a 'girl.' After a little discussion about the work, privileges, etc., and upon the production of some written certificates--it is almost impossible to obtain personal references, and if it were possible you could not rely upon them--the engagement is made. The mistress requires a solemn promise that the servant will come on a certain day, and as often as not the day arrives without her. Our young lady has been round to a number of mistresses and 'priced' their places; she will not wilfully put you in a quandary, but if, after having engaged herself to you, she hears of another situation where there is less work or more wages, she takes it in preference, and leaves you to manage as best you can. Even when you have got her and found her suitable, you can never tell at what moment she will be pleased to be off 'Tuppence more and up goes the donkey!'--an inconvenience which is felt much more here, where there is probably only one servant in the house, than it would be in England.

But if it were only higher wages which tempted servants away the remedy would be easy; a few pounds more a year would be cheerfully paid for the convenience of a continuity of one's household arrangements. In one year we have had ten servants. As there were no children, the place was an easy one; but that seemed to make little difference. At first we kept two, but they did nothing but quarrel; the cook left us on this account. We took our new cook simply because she happened to be a friend of the housemaid; but before long we found that it was out of the frying-pan into the fire: the first two had quarrelled 'because there wasn't sufficient work for two to do;' the second pair played together so much that they never did any work. We banished them both, and tried keeping only one servant, which many people had assured us would prove more comfortable. So far they were right. Hitherto my wife's time had chiefly been taken up with looking after the servants, to see that they did their work; now peace reigned in the house. We gave our maid-of-all-work fifteen shillings a week; we thought we had found a real treasure, and for a month everything went on wheels. But at the end of that time, just when she was getting accustomed to our ways and we to hers, Sarah gives a week's notice; she had no fault to find with her mistress, but the place was too dull. We offered two shillings a week extra but in vain. Our next stayed six weeks; her reason for leaving was that she did not approve of the back-yard. Number six stayed for three months; she was very nearly leaving at the end of the first fortnight, but we won her heart by giving her young man free access to the kitchen from 9 o'clock to 10.30 every evening. Even then, however, she found the place too dull. Number eight stayed two months; she left avowedly because she did not care to stop too long in one place. The ninth remained only a fortnight. She left because we objected to her staying out after eleven o'clock at night, although we gave her three nights out a week after half-past eight.

When there are children in a middle-class family, a nurse-girl is generally, but by, no means always, kept. Hers is the lowest of all the branches of service, and is only taken by a young girl just going out into the world. Trained nurses, such as are common at home, are in great demand, and almost unobtainable. They can earn a pound a week easily, and at such wages a man whose income only runs into three figures is forced to put up with a nurse-girl. She undertakes no responsibility, her duties being confined to carrying the baby and screaming at the other children if they attempt to do themselves any bodily harm. If you wish to understand what the average nurse-girl is like, you have but to walk through any of the public gardens; you will see babies without number left in the blazing sun, some hanging half-way out of their perambulators, others sucking large, painted 'lollies' or green apples. The elder children, if they are unruly, are slapped and sent off to play by themselves, while the nurse-girls hold a confab on a neighbouring bench. Not that these girls are necessarily bad, but they lack the supervision and training of a head-nurse; they have been taught to look upon nursing as derogatory, and never stay long enough as nurses to get an experience in handling children. A few months of this, the lowest stage of servant-galdom, and then they pass up into the maid-of-all-work class. Thus it is that many mothers prefer undertaking the duties of nurse themselves, and devote themselves to their children often at the expense of their husbands, and certainly of all social relations.

Colonial servants are much too fond of change for change's sake ever to stay long in one situation. A month's character is a sure guarantee for another place, and only a week's notice is required on either side before leaving. Hence servants are engaged and paid by the week; they do not expect any presents or perquisites, and it is not the custom to make them any allowance for beer. On the other hand, they will not stand being allowanced for tea, sugar, butter, or anything of the kind, and as a rule they fare in exactly the same style as their masters. Every other Sunday afternoon and evening, one evening every week, and occasional public holidays, are the customary outings, though we found it expedient to allow a good many more.

The great redeeming-point about the servant-girl is the power she acquires, of getting through a large and multifarious quantity of work. She has frequently to do the whole house-work, cooking, washing, and ironing for a family of six or seven, and unless the mistress or her daughters are particularly helpful, it is out of all reason to expect that any of these things can be well done. Of course there are some good servants, but, unfortunately for their employers, the butchers and bakers generally have a keen eye for such, arguing with great justice that a good servant is likely to make a good wife.

The greater part of the high wages which servants get is spent on dress. If ever they condescend to wear their mistress's left-off clothes, it is only for work in the house; but the trouble they take to copy the exact fashion and cut of their mistress's clothes is very amusing. One girl we had frankly asked my wife to allow her to take a dress she admired to her dressmaker, in order that she might have one made up like it. Whilst girls in the upper and middle classes are very handy with their fingers, and often make up their own hats and dresses, the servant-class despise to do this, and almost invariably employ milliners, who often cheat them dreadfully, knowing that they appreciate a hat or a dress much according to the price they have paid for it, and the amount of show it makes. In hats and bonnets this is specially noticeable; I have often seen our servants with hats or bonnets on, which cannot have cost them less than three or four pounds.

The shortest and upon the whole the best way to get a servant is by going to one of the numerous registry offices. Some of these exist merely to palm off bad servants upon you; but there are always offices of good reputation, which will not recommend a girl they know absolutely nothing about.

The needlewoman is little in vogue here; but as nearly everyone washes at home, washerwomen are plentiful; their wages run from four to five shillings a day, according to their capabilities, food being of course included.

In spite of constant shipments from England, servants are always at a premium, and I need scarcely point out what an excellent opening these colonies afford for women-servants. Unfortunately, but a very small proportion of the daughters of the poorer colonial working-class will go into service. For some inexplicable reason, they turn up their noses at the high wages and comparatively light work offered, and prefer to undertake the veriest drudgery in factories for a miserable pittance. At a recent strike in a large shirt-making factory in Melbourne, it came out that a competent needlewoman could not make more than eighteen shillings a week even by working overtime, and that the general average earnings of a factory girl were only eleven to thirteen shillings a week. But so great is the love of independence in the colonial girl, that she prefers hard work and low wages in order to be able to enjoy freedom of an evening. It is in vain that the press points out that girls whose parents do not keep servants are accustomed to perform the same household duties in their own homes that are required of them in service; that work which is not degrading at home cannot be degrading in service; and that they will be the better wives for the knowledge of household work which they acquire in service. They might as well preach to the winds; and there are more applications for employment in shops and factories than there is work for, whilst mistresses go begging for lady-helps. There is a sad side to this picture as regards the social condition of the colonies, in addition to the inconvenience to people who keep servants. The girls who go into shops and factories, and have their evenings to themselves, necessarily undergo a great deal of temptation, and it is undeniable that they are not at all delivered from evil. The subject is out of keeping with these letters, but unless some means can be found to reconcile colonial girls to service, I fear an evil is growing up in our midst which is likely to be even more baneful in its effects upon the community than the corresponding tendency to 'larrikinism' amongst colonial youths.

Since writing the above, an article on the subject has appeared in the Melbourne *Argus* which is worth quoting in *extenso*:

'We have undertaken to consider whether anything can be done to overcome the unwillingness which nearly all Australian girls exhibit to enter domestic service. There is an abundant supply of female labour in the colony, but unfortunately it is not distributed in the way that would be most advantageous to the community and beneficial to the women themselves. While household servants can scarcely be had for love or money, the clothing factories are crowded with seamstresses, who are content to work long hours at what are very much like starvation wages. How is this? We have shown that there is nothing in domestic work which any true woman need consider degrading; that the most refined and highly educated ladies have in all ages considered themselves properly employed when busy about household affairs; that servants have quite as many opportunities of forming matrimonial connections as factory girls, and that their training fits them to become much better, and therefore far happier wives. We have no doubt that all this, or at least the greater part, would be admitted by the seamstresses themselves: but nevertheless the fact remains that to domestic service they will not go. There is a feeling in existence amongst them that in some way or other household labour is menial occupation, and that to undertake it is to lose caste in the class to which they belong. We may call this fantastic idea "vanity" or "false pride," or what we will; but that does not do anything to banish it, or to render it less potent for mischief. Seeing that so much is at stake--that employers are clamouring for servants, and that women are sadly in want of some occupation which would lessen competition and raise wages in the sewing business--it is evident that society is deeply interested in getting rid of the ridiculous notion. As a first step towards that desirable consummation, let us endeavour to analyse the impression which exists in the minds of those who turn their backs upon household duties, and with their eyes open devote themselves to a laborious and underpaid occupation.

'A correspondent (*The Argus*, December 16) informs us that observation and the remarks he has heard made by factory girls have led him to think that there are three serious objections which the seamstresses have to domestic service. One of these is--"The idea of degradation, attached to the position of a 'slavey' in the minds of the lower classes themselves." As we have seen that there is nothing degrading in the work itself which servants are called upon to do, how comes it that its performance is considered less honourable than sewing or serving in a shop? The notion must take its rise in the conditions under which domestic service is rendered. The sewing girl or the shop-woman has certain business hours, outside of which she is as independent as her employer, and as little amenable to control. The household servant, on the other hand, is under discipline, and liable to be called on to do this, that, or the other during every hour of the twenty-four. From the time she gets up in the morning to the moment she goes to bed at night, she has no hour which of right she can reckon on as her own. If she wishes to go out she must ask permission; if she wants to receive a friend, she cannot rely on being left undisturbed. As a matter of fact, servants in this colony enjoy a very large measure of liberty, and those who are worth their salt very seldom have to complain of want of consideration or indulgence. If they do not meet with proper treatment, they can easily find situations where more regard is had to their feelings and comfort. But the thought that the leisure and freedom they enjoy is due in a great measure to favour, and not to right, is the fly in the ointment of the domestic's lot which renders it distasteful to many women, and which causes it to be looked down on by those who exist under far less favourable conditions. It seems to us that it is the want of some definite respite from liability to work which constitutes the "slavery" of which our correspondent speaks. If we are right in our supposition, then it is evident that employers have it in their power to take away the reproach from domestic servitude, by assimilating the conditions of household employment to those which attach to industrial occupations. Why should not servants have regular hours of work, outside which they would be absolutely free to go where, or to do as they please, without asking permission or fearing interruption? If such arrangements were to become customary, we can hardly doubt that the prejudice against domestic service would die out. The attractions of higher wages, equal freedom, better board, and more comfortable lodging would soon do their work.

'It may be said that such a change as we propose would entirely alter the relations between mistresses and their "helps." No doubt it would. But we may ask why the relations between mistresses and servants should continue as they were in semi-feudal times, when the relations of other classes of society to each other have been resettled on an entirely different basis? Nearly all sorts of service now are matters of simple contract, and we know of no reason why domestic engagements should not be regulated in the same way. It would be better for employers to have a plentiful supply of efficient servants liable to work eight or ten hours per diem, than a scanty stock of discontented women whose services they can command day and night. With altered relations, we should soon have a change of demeanour on both sides. The correspondent we have quoted says that another of the things which prevents seamstresses from "going into service," is "the over-anxiety of mistresses that servants should know their position." In a democratic country like this, where young people are brought up with the idea that one man or woman is as good as another, we can easily understand that any assertion of superiority on the part of employers, or attempt to exact an outward show of deference, is very galling to undisciplined minds. Those who have been accustomed to be waited on from childhood upwards, are never very careful to insist on those forms and modes of address which at one time servants invariably adopted. As long as they are well served, they are content to sacrifice something to the modern spirit of equality. It is those who have risen in the social scale late in life who are always standing on their dignity and exacting homage. If the latter class would moderate its pretensions, a stumbling-block would be removed from the entrance to domestic service. We already have several agencies for training servants; could they not add to their duties the work of training mistresses in the ideas we have set forth, and in any others which are likely to diminish the distaste of Australian girls for household work? If they would take the matter in hand in a practical way, and familiarise the public mind with the notion of limited domestic labour, they would, we believe, do much to promote the comfort of home life in Victoria, and to improve the position of female labour.'

FOOD.

Generally speaking, food in Australia is cheaper and more plentiful than in England, but poorer in quality. Adulteration is, of course, as yet unknown, or but very little known, for the simple reason that it costs more to adulterate than to provide the genuine article. The working-man's food here is also immeasurably better and cheaper. Mutton he gets almost for the asking, and up-country almost without it. Bread is only 1¼d. to 2d. a pound, and all the necessaries of life are good, healthy, and fairly cheap. But the richer man, who asks for more than soundness in the quality of his food, finds himself worse off than in London. Meat of the same quality as he gets at his club in Pall Mall is not to be got in Collins Street for love or money. The flour is the best in the world, and the bread wholesome and sweet; but the toothsomeness of German and French bakers is not to be had, and the finest qualities of flour are all shipped to England instead of being used here. The dearness of labour makes it impossible to give the same care to the cultivation of fruit and vegetables; and though these are cheap enough, the delicate flavour of Convent Garden is hardly compensated by their superior freshness. In short, our food is somewhat coarse, albeit wholesome enough.

Up-country the meat is excellent; but in the towns it is not, as a rule, so good as in England, as the sheep and cattle have often to be driven long distances before they are slaughtered. Prices vary according to the different towns, seasons, and qualities from 6d. to 2½d. a lb. for beef, and from 4d. to 1½d. for mutton. Pork is from 9d. to 7d.; veal from 8d. to 4d. All kinds of fruit and vegetables, except Brussels sprouts, are cheap and plentiful. I will quote one or two prices at random from a market-book: artichokes, 1½d. a lb.; tomatoes, 2d. a lb.; beetroot and cabbages, 1s. 6d. a dozen; potatoes, 6s. a cwt. During the season fruit is very cheap. Splendid Muscatel grapes can be bought in Adelaide from 1d. to 2d. a lb.; peaches, 3d. a dozen; apricots, 2d. a dozen; raspberries, 5d. a lb.; cherries, 2d. a lb.; strawberries, 4d.; plums almost for nothing; but by far the best is the passion-fruit. Neither vegetables nor fruit, as sold in the markets and shops, are as good as those you buy in England. The inferior quality is due to the grow-as-you-please manner in which the fruit is cultivated, pruning and even the most ordinary care being neglected; but you can get as fine-flavoured fruit here as anywhere, and to taste grapes in perfection you must certainly go to Adelaide.

Of course meat is the staple of Australian life. A working-man whose whole family did not eat meat three times a day would indeed be a phenomenon. High and low rich and poor, all eat meat to an incredible extent, even in the hottest weather. Not that they know how to prepare it in any delicate way, for to the working and middle, as well as to most of the wealthy classes, cooking is an unknown art. The meat is roast or boiled, hot or cold, sometimes fried or hashed. It is not helped in mere slices, but in good substantial hunks. In everything the colonist likes quantity. You can hardly realize the delight of 'tucking in' to a dish of fruit at a dinner-party. I once heard a colonist say, 'I don't like your nasty little English slices of meat: *we* want something that we can put our teeth into.' Imagine the man's misery when dessert came on the table, and he was asked whether he would take a *slice* of pear! Vegetables are for the most part despised, though the thoroughly old English dish of greens remains in favour, and potatoes are largely eaten.

Tea may fairly claim to be the national beverage. A large majority of the population drink it with every meal, and you find cases of this even in the metropolitan middle classes. With them, however, it is more usual to drink beer with their mid-day meal, and to have meat-tea in the evening. This practice extends through the upper and middle classes, and into many wealthy houses. Next to tea may be ranked beer, English or colonial, which I have come to think is a necessity to the English-speaking races. But no colonist drinks much at meals. He prefers to quench his thirst at every opportunity that may occur between. In all country towns, if you go to see a man on business, out comes the whisky-bottle. If you meet an old friend, his first greeting is, 'Come and have a nobbler!' No bargain can be concluded without it. If it is a warm day, you must have a nobbler to quench your thirst; if it is freezing, to keep the cold out. There is no trade at which more fortunes have been made here than the publican's. The most exclusive and the most out-at-elbows find a common meeting-place in the public-house; although it is only fair to say that the custom of 'shouting,' as it is called, is going--if it has not gone--out of fashion amongst the better classes in the capital cities. Beer, or more frequently spirits, form the favourite 'nobbler,' the price of which varies from fourpence to eightpence in Sydney and Adelaide according to the drink. In Melbourne all drinks are sixpence. There is a current story--which I know to be true--of two well-known colonials, who, on landing from the P. and O. steamer at Southampton, immediately entered the first public-house, and asked for 'two nobblers of English ale.' Having drunk the ale, which was highly approved of, one of them put down a shilling, and was walking off, when the barmaid recalled him, and offered eightpence change. 'By G----!' was their simultaneous exclamation, 'this is a land to live in, where you can get two nobblers of English ale for fourpence! let us drink our shilling's-worth.'

Like their American cousins, the Australians are of opinion that there is no liquid worthy to be mentioned by the side of 'champagne.' It requires some education to acquire a taste for claret. To the uninitiated sherry and port are chiefly palatable for their spirituousness; but everyone is born with a taste for champagne. It does not follow that everyone knows what constitutes good champagne. No merchant or lawyer, or anyone whose income is over

£500 a year, dare give a party without champagne. It is champagne which gives *ton*. For this purpose it need not be very good.

The *sine quibus non* are a well-known brand and a 'gold-top.' Moët's or Roëderer's *carte d'or* is the party-goer's criterion of the success of the entertainment. As soon as he sees the label, he swallows the wine, good or bad--more probably bad, for most champagnes, like all other wines, are 'specially prepared for the Australian market,' and you know what that means. 'Body,' or what captious folk would call 'heaviness,' is the first condition of good wine to the colonial taste. The lower middle and lower classes also like it sweet; but of course a man who drinks any quantity of wine prefers it dry. Besides the champagne drunk for show, there is--in spite of a 20s. a dozen duty--a large quantity consumed in the way of nobblers, and at dinner by wealthy men. When a man has made a lucky speculation, or has just got a large order, he treats his friends to a bottle of champagne.

I have not seen burgundy half a dozen times since I have been here. The old colonist finds claret thin and sour; but the younger generation are beginning to take to it, although there is no wine harder to obtain here than claret. Nine-tenths of what one buys is adulterated. His knowledge of *crûs* being naturally limited, the colonist likes to see on his wine a fine label, one which makes the quality of the wine easily comprehensible to him. Thus the most successful claret sold here is divided according to degrees of nastiness into five ranks, and you ask for So-and-So's No. 0, 1, 2, 3, 4, irrespective of vintage or year. 'Bon ordinaire' is of course unobtainable, but you can get 'Chateau Margaux,' duty paid, at from 40s. to 50s. a dozen. I was once asked to buy some wine bearing that label for 2s. 6d. a bottle. The names of one or two well-known wines having reached your host's ears, he likes to show you by the name on the label that he is giving them to you; and, unfortunately, Margaux and Lafitte *labels* cost no more than any other.

A good deal of sherry and port--even more brandied than for the English market--is drunk. A wealthy man will never give you colonial wine, not because it is necessarily worse than the imported stuff on his table, but because it is colonial. Amongst the middle classes it is beginning to find favour. A great deal of extravagant praise has been lavished in the press on these wines since the Bordeaux Exhibition, and I fear that many who taste them for the first time will be disappointed. They are too heady, and for the most part wanting in bouquet, whilst their distinctive character repels the palate, which is accustomed to European growths. But for all that, I cannot understand how men with only moderate means living out here can pay large prices for very inferior imported wines, when a good sound, palatable wine is obtainable at from 15s. to 25s. a dozen. At the latter price a Sauvignon approaching to claret, grown close to Melbourne, is obtainable, which is really excellent; and the white hermitage from the same district, as well as from the Hunter River district in New South Wales, at 15s. a dozen, is also as good as one can wish, short of a *grand vin*, although in none of these wines do you entirely lose the *goût du terroir*, a peculiar earthy taste resulting from the strength of the soil. The cheapest wholesome wine I have ever drunk off the Continent is a thin *vin ordinaire*, smelling like *piquette*, which is sold at a certain rather low-looking shop in Melbourne. It is quite palatable, and when heavily watered I can vouch for its wholesomeness.

The lightest of these wines contain about 18 degrees of spirit, whereas, as you know, an 'ordinaire' has only about 8, and a burgundy not more than 11 or 12. But the native wines which are generally preferred by the colonists themselves are the South Australian. In spite of a duty of 10s. a dozen, large quantities of Adelaide wine are drunk in Melbourne. Its chief characteristics are sweetness and heaviness. It may seem to you incredible, but I have drunk a wine made from the Verdeilho grape, and, grown near Adelaide by a Mr. C. Bonney, which contained no less than 36 degrees of natural spirit, without a drop added: 32 and 33 degrees are quite common, and the average percentage in South Australian wine is about 28.

In most cases the wines are named after the grape from which they are made, though sometimes the less sensible course of calling the wine 'claret,' 'sherry,' or 'port,' is adopted. I say less sensible, because all colonial wines have a peculiar flavour, which makes it difficult to mistake them for the wines they profess to imitate. The Carbinet-Sauvignon grape, which I believe is the principal one used in the Bordeaux district, produces here a wine something like what you get on the Rhone. The Riesling, a Rhineland grape, resembles a brandied hock; it makes one of the best wines, and is often very palatable. The red and white Hermitage grapes do best of all. The Muscatel makes a delicious sweet wine in Adelaide, but it is very heady. I have no doubt that in the course of time, and when more scientific methods are pursued, South Australia will produce excellent ports and sherries, as well as Constantias, Malagas, and madeira, but I fear it will not be within the present generation. Claret, I understand from experts, will never be produced, but hermitages and wines of that type will be made in the course of ten or twenty years which will be able to compete in the European markets; long before this they should become useful for blending with French and Spanish wines. As a rule the wine is already sound and wholesome; and if one comes to think of it, taste is a purely arbitrary matter. One forms one's taste according to a certain standard to which one is accustomed. To a man accustomed to colonial wines, clarets and hocks seem thin and sour. One great difficulty which militates against the reputation of Australian wine, is that of the untrustworthiness of all but a few brands. Of course all vintages from the same grapes differ, but there is a margin of difference beyond which a wine may not go, and with many an Australian *vigneron* this margin is frequently passed, owing to carelessness or inexperience in manufacture. Another drawback is the difficulty of procuring all but the most immature wine. Nearly the whole of each vintage is drunk within twelve months after it is made. That Australian wines will ever compete with the famous French *crûs* I should very much doubt, but that they will in the course of the next twenty years gradually supersede with advantage a great deal of the manufactured stuff now drunk in England is more than probable. At present the prices are too high for Australian wines to find any large market at home. Although it is of course an exceptional case, there is an Adelaide madeira which fetches as much as 63s. per dozen within two miles of the vineyard. Nothing now obtainable in Australia under 15s. a dozen would be worth sending home, and by the time freight and duty is added to that, the London price would be considerable.

I have already made allusion to that peculiar phase of Australian life--nobblerising; but, if I am not mistaken, the impression left on your mind will be that the nobbler is either of aristocratic champagne or plebeian beer. But there are two other liquids--whisky and brandy--which play an important part in nobblerising. The quantity of spirits drunk in Australia is appalling. Whisky is the favourite spirit, then brandy, and rarely Schiedam, schnapps, or gin. And what about drunkenness? Statistically it is not very much worse than in England, but the difference lies in the class who get drunk. Here it is not merely the lower classes, but everybody that drinks. Not a few of the wealthiest and most leading citizens are well-known to be frequently drunk, though their names do not, of course, appear in the papers or in the police reports. The state of public feeling on the subject, though improving, is much as it was in England twenty or thirty years ago. Society says, 'Capital fellow, Jones; pity he drinks!' but no social reprobation attaches to Jones. He may be known to be carried to bed every night, for all it affects his reputation as a respectable and respected citizen. But with the advance of civilization better times are coming in these matters. It is no more so absolute a necessity to take a nobbler as it was ten years ago. Drunkenness, if not reprobated, is no longer considered a 'gentlemanly vice.' A man who drinks is pitied. This is the first step. Before long blame will tread in the steps of pity.

But enough of drinking. It is not a pleasant subject. Besides, I have not yet described the food of any but the working-class. And if they live ten times better than their fellows at home, it is equally true that the middle, and especially the upper, class live ten times worse. It requires the tongue and the pen of a Brillat-Savarin to give flavour to a Barmecide's feast; but as victualling is as necessary a condition of existence here as anywhere else, I must do my best to enlighten you as to our situation in this respect. May you never have practical experience thereof! If it be true that, while the French eat, the English only feed, we may fairly add that the Australians 'grub'. Nor could it well be otherwise under the circumstances. It is not merely because it is difficult to entice a good cook to come out here. If he really wants a thing, the wealthy colonist will not spare money to get it; but how can you expect a man who--for the greater part of his life--has been eating mutton and damper, and drinking parboiled tea three times a day, to understand the art of good living? Even if he does, he finds it unappreciated by those around him; and there are few men fond enough of the luxuries of life to be singular in their enjoyment. It takes a lot of trouble to get and keep a good cook, and there is nothing the Australian abhors like trouble. Consequently--I am now speaking only of the wealthy--he adopts one of two courses.

Either he gives occasional grand dinners, in which case he imagines he has got a good cook because he is paying £60 or £70 a year for him--no very large salary even in England for a *chef*; or he is contented to live anyhow. In the latter case he dines at his club (where, by the way, he gets a very fair meal) in the middle of the day, and has meat-tea in the evening. In both cases the family dinner is much the same. No. 1 cannot see the use of having what he would call a 'spread' for his own selfish benefit, and leaves his grand cook unemployed the greater part of the week. The dinner consists of beef or mutton, roast or boiled, potatoes and greens, bread-and-butter pudding, and cheese. The details change, but the type is always the same--what his wife calls 'a good plain English dinner, none of your unwholesome French kickshaws,' which are reserved for company. Fortunately his cook, if not very expert in the 'foreign' dishes required to be concocted for company, has generally pretty correct notions within the limits of the family dinner.

But it is not so with No. 2, and with the large middle class who all live in the same way. The usual female cook at 12s. a week is not even capable of sending up a plain meal properly. Her meat is tough, and her potatoes are watery. Her pudding-range extends from rice to sago, and from sago to rice, and in many middle-class households pudding is reserved for Sundays and visitors. A favourite summer dish is stewed fruit, and, as it is not easy to make it badly, there is a great deal to commend in it. At the worst, it is infinitely preferable to fruit tart with an indigestible crust.

Ye gentlemen of England, who sit at home at ease, how astonished you would be to see your daughter Maud, whose husband is a well-to-do lawyer in considerable practice, setting the table herself because she cannot rely upon her servant doing it properly! And then she goes into the kitchen, and teaches cook how to make pie-crust. If children are numerous, or her husband is not getting on quite so well as could be wished, she will not be able to have a servant to wait at table. What wonder, then, if she gives up late dinner and has a meat-tea, at which everything can be put on the table at once. A colonial-bred lady has generally learnt something of good plain cooking, but the English mistress often breaks down before the serious and multifarious nature of her duties. It is by no means uncommon for her to be suddenly left servantless for two or three days; and if she does not possess great adaptability of disposition, the whole house is bound to be at sixes-and-sevens, and all its occupants, including herself, in anything but a pleasant state of mind. If a woman is worth her salt, she will not mind these things, or rather she will make the best of them; but it is not every English young lady whose love for her husband, present or future, will carry her through these domestic hurricanes; and, if not, she had better not come out here, although husbands are plentiful. Except amongst a very small class who can afford luxuries, the girl-of-the-period is out of place in Australia.

DRESS.

I doubt whether in my preceding letters I have made the distinction between Melbourne and its sister capitals sufficiently plain. I shall perhaps best convey it by saying that Melbourne is quasi-metropolitan, while both Sydney and Adelaide are alike provincial in their mode of life. In the matters of which I have been writing, the difference has hardly been sufficient to warrant a separate treatment; but with regard to dress, it becomes so noticeable, that not to treat of Melbourne separately would convey a false idea. For in dress it is not too much to say that the ladies of Melbourne are luxurious-a charge which could scarcely be brought against Australians in any other particular that I can think of. And take them all-in-all, they do not dress badly; indeed, if one considers the distance from Paris, and the total want of a competent leader of fashion, they may be said to dress well, especially of late years. The highly fantastic and gorgeous costumes for which Melbourne used to be notorious are fast disappearing. Successful diggers no longer take their wives into a shop, and ask how much colour and stuff can be put into a dress for fifty pounds. Already outrageousness is confined to a few, and when I say that it is generally agreed to be 'bad form,' you will understand that its death-blow has been struck and the hearse ordered. Bright colours are still in vogue, but they are not necessarily loud or unpleasant beneath the austral sun, and the act of combining them is beginning to be understood. When one remembers how their houses are furnished, and what their general style of living is it is astonishing to find Melbourne ladies dressing so brilliantly and yet with so little vulgarity.

But it is not among the *grand monde*--if the term be not ridiculous as applied to Victoria--that you must go to discover taste. I am not sure that, class for class, the rich do not show the least taste in their apparel. Many of them send to Paris for their dresses, and pay sums, which make one's mouth water, to be dressed in the latest fashion; but I fancy that the French *modistes* manufacture a certain style of attire for the Australian taste, just as the French merchants manufacture clarets for the Australian market. It is a compound of the *cocotte* and the American. Nor when she has got a handsome dress does the Melbourne *grande dame* know how to wear it; she merely succeeds in looking what a Brighton lodging-house keeper once defined to me as a 'carriage-lady.' A lady of the English upper middle-class dressed by a London milliner looks infinitely better.

There are some costumes worn by Victorian ladies which you will never see worn by any other ladies; but for all that, the middle and even the lower class am by no means destitute of ideas about dress. Compare the Melbourne with the Birmingham or Manchester factory girl, or the young lady in a Collins Street retail establishment with the shop-girl in any but the most aristocratic part of London; the old country will come out second-best. And why is it? It is no easy question to answer; at the bottom is undoubtedly that general love of display, which is almost as characteristic of Melbourne as it is of Paris. But then what is the cause of that? And a love of display, though it may be and is amongst the wealthy productive of grand dresses, as it is of grand dinners and grand furniture, does not make taste--e.g., the Second Empire; and though it would be going too far to say that the ladies of Melbourne dress tastefully, it is within the truth to give them credit for a tendency towards taste. Throughout England the middle and lower classes dress hideously. Why should the first generation of Victorians show a disposition to abandon the ugly? I leave it to some aesthetic philosopher to find out the reason, and content myself with noting the fact. If I wanted to moralize, I have little doubt that the drapers' and milliners' accounts of these 'young ladies' would furnish a redundant text, and that, although a large number of them make up their dresses themselves from paper patterns or illustrations in *Myra's Journal*. How they can afford to dress as well as they do, they and their mothers best know; but the bow here and the flower there are not costly things, and the mere fact of being able to cut out a dress so as not to look dowdy shows natural taste. It is the rarest of sights to see a real Melbourne girl look dowdy. Her taste sometimes runs riot: it is exuberant, and becomes vulgar and flash; but even then the vulgarity and flashness are of a superior type to those of her equals across the ocean.

Sydney and Adelaide are distinctly superior to English towns of the same size in the matter of apparel; but they will not bear comparison with Melbourne. On the other hand, gorgeous and flash dresses are very rare in the smaller cities. If they have not the talent of Melbourne, neither do they share its blots. They go along at a steady jog-trot, and are content to take their fashions second-hand from Melbourne, but with modifications. Their more correct and sober taste will not tolerate even many of the extravagances of which London is guilty--such extravagances, for instance, as the Tam O'Shanter cap, which was warmly taken up in Melbourne. But with all this good sense, they remain dowdy.

I have said nothing hitherto of married ladies' dress. When a colonial girl marries, she considers herself, except in rare instances, on the shelf, and troubles herself very little about what she wears. As a rule, she has probably too many other things to take up her time. She has got a husband, and what more can she want? He rarely cares what she has on, as soon as the honeymoon is over. There is no one else to please, and I fear that colonial girls are not of those who dress merely for themselves; they like to be admired, and they appreciate the value of dress from a flirtation point of view. Their taste is rather the outcome of a desire to please others than of a sense of aesthetics. It is relative, and not absolute. When once the finery has served its purpose, they are ready to renounce all the pomps and vanities of this wicked world. And if the moralist says that this argues some laxness of ideas before marriage, let him remember that it is equally indicative of connubial bliss. Once married, her flirtations are at an end--'played out,' if I may use the term.

In another respect the Victorian is the direct opposite of the *Parisienne*. If you leave general effects, and come to pull her dress to pieces, you find that the metal is only electro, to whatever rank of life she may belong. The general appearance may be pleasing, but in detail she is execrable. Not but that the materials of her dress are rich enough, so that my electro simile will hardly hold water; but money does not make the artist. Let us begin with the bonnet. Walk down Collins Street at the time of the block on Saturday, and I doubt whether you can count half a dozen bonnets which are both pretty and suitable to the face and head of the wearer. *Bien chaussée et bien gantée* might be Greek as far as Australia is concerned, and if by chance you see a stocking or any portion of the under-clothing, you will have your eyes opened. Whatever does not meet the eye is generally of the commonest. It would be thought a sinful waste of money to have anything particularly good or expensive which other people could not see. The light of Melbourne is never likely to hide itself under a bushel; external adornment is the *mot d'ordre*. Ribbons and laces, or anything that helps to improve the look of a dress, the colonial lady will indulge in freely and even extravagantly; but you must not penetrate her tinsel armour.

Owing to the climate, hats are much more frequently in use than bonnets, and if the merit of subdued tints is unappreciated, it is not often that the eye is shocked by the glaring discords to which Englishwomen are so prone. Fringes are much worn, and the hair is often parted on the side. In spite of the heat, *gants de suède* find very little favour; they look dirty, and with a 25 per cent. duty cannot be renewed every day. The usual English fashions find their way to Melbourne in about eight months, and this is the more convenient, because your summer is our winter, and *vice versa*. Spring and autumn we agree to forget; this is rather a pity, because practically nine-twelfths of our year are spring and autumn, and on a bright July or August day the dress which is appropriate to a London fog in December looks singularly out of place. Sealskins and furs are worn till you almost imagine it must be cold, which during daylight it hardly ever is in this country. In summer, suitable concessions become obligatory, and dresses are made of the thinnest and lightest materials. Pompadour prints and white calicoes reign supreme, and look better than anything else. It is then that the poorer classes are able to dress best, the material being cheap. Winter stuffs are expensive, and to a great degree their effectiveness is in direct ratio to their cost; but during quite half of the Australian year the poor meet the rich, if not on an equality, at any rate on much fairer terms than at home with regard to dress.

Servants, of course, ape their mistresses' dresses as in England, and generally manage to produce a delightful sense of incongruity in their attire; but for all that, they are much less dowdy than English servants.

So much for ladies' dress. Change the sexes, and the picture is by no means so pleasing; for thorough untidiness of person, there can surely be no one to beat the Australian. Above all must one beware of judging a man's position by his coat. It is impossible to tell whether the dirty old man who slouches along the street is a millionaire or a beggar. The older his coat, and the dirtier his shirt, the more the probabilities are in favour of the millionaire. Perhaps he thinks he can afford to dress as he pleases. The city men are more careful of their personal appearance, and have kept up the shadow and image of London. They wear shiny frock-coats and the worst-brushed and most odd-shaped of top-hats, and imagine they are well-dressed; at least I suppose they do, for they seem to have a sort of contempt for the spruce tweed suits and round hats of 'new chums,' and such of the rising generation as have followed their example and adopted that fashion. Can you imagine yourself wearing a black coat and high hat with the thermometer jogging about from 70° to 110° in the shade? If the coat were decently cut, and of good cloth and well-brushed, and the silk hat well-shapen and neat, I might put you down a fool, but would admit your claims to be a dandy. But as it is, most of our city men are both uncomfortable and untidy. Their clothes look as if they had been bought ready-made at a slop-shop. The tie they prefer is a black bootlace; if not, it is bound to be of the most tasteless colour and pattern you can think of. A heavy gold watch-chain and diamond ring is *de rigueur*, but otherwise they do not wear much jewellery. Their hair, like their clothes, generally wants brushing, and hands and nails are not always so clean as they might be; but one knows that for the most part they tub every morning: this is a consolation.

The bushman, at least, dresses sensibly. Wen he comes into town, he puts on a slop-coat, but retains, if not a cabbage-tree, at any rate a wide-brimmed, soft felt hat. Sacrificing comfort to ceremony, he generally puts on a collar, but he often kicks at a tie: he finds he must draw a line somewhere. But there is something so redolent of the bush about him, that one would not have him otherwise; the slop clothes even become picturesque from the cavalier fashion in which he wears them. Note that his pipe never leaves his mouth, while the city man does not venture to smoke in any of the main streets. He is a regular Jack ashore, this bushman. A bull would not be more out of place in a china-shop, though probably less amusing and more destructive. The poor fellow meets so many friends in town, that by the end of the day he has probably had more nobblers than are altogether good for him. It is a very hard life that he leads, and he takes his pleasure, like his work, hardly.

If the Adelaidians are perhaps the least got-up, they are certainly the most suitably dressed of the inhabitants of Australian towns. With them the top hat is comparatively of recent introduction. Silk coats and helmets are numerous still, though becoming more rare every day. Melbourne and Sydney think it *infra dig.* to allow themselves these little comforts, and Adelaide is gradually becoming corrupted. It must, however, be added that the Adelaide folk are the most untidy, as the Melbourne are the least untidy of Australians. Comfort and elegance do not always go hand in hand. Tweeds are beginning to come into use amongst the upper middle, as they long have in the lower middle and lower classes. Capital stuffs are made at Sydney, Melbourne, Ballarat, and Geelong; but the patterns are very common. In a dusty place like this it is impossible to keep black clothes clean, and tweeds give far the best wear and appearance of any stuff. For my own part, I wear them winter and summer.

The working-classes can, of course, afford to be, and are, better dressed than at home; for though clothes are in reality much dearer, they are much cheaper in proportion to wages. They do not often wear black coats in the week, but keep them for Sundays and grand occasions. Directly an immigrant has landed, he feels that his first earnings must be devoted to a Sunday go-to-meeting suit. His fellow-men all have one, and he does not like to feel himself their inferior, even with regard to a coat.

YOUNG AUSTRALIA.

Hitherto I have been writing of the properties and adjuncts of Australian life. It is high time to say something of the colonists themselves. And, here I shall describe the types which the colony has produced and is producing, rather than such modifications as colonists born and bred in England have undergone during their subsequent residence in Australia--colonials as distinct from colonists.

Perhaps of their first stage of existence the less said the better. I have a holy horror of babies, to whatever nationality they may belong; but for general objectionableness I believe there are none to compare with the Australian baby. It is not only that the summer heat and sudden changes of climate make him worse-behaved than his *confrères* over the ocean, but the little brute is omnipresent, and I might almost add omnipotent. Nurses are more expensive and mothers less fastidious than in England. Consequently, baby lives in the family circle almost from the time of its birth. Nurseries are few and far between. He is lashed into a chair by his mother's side at meals; he accompanies her when she is attending to her household duties, and often even when she is receiving her visitors. But if this were all I would say nothing. French children are brought up in a similar way; and in their case it certainly has its advantages as far as the child is concerned, whatever may be the inconvenience to the adults amongst whom it is brought. It is easy to avoid families whose children make themselves nuisances to visitors. But the middle and lower classes of Australians are not content with the baby's supremacy in the household. Wherever his mother goes, baby is also taken. He fills railway carriages and omnibuses, obstructs the pavement in perambulators, and is suckled *coram populo* in the Exhibition. There is no getting away from him, unless you shut yourself up altogether. He squalls at concerts; you have to hold him while his mother gets out of the omnibus, and to kiss him if you are visiting her house.

It is little better when he gets old enough to walk and talk. Having once made the household bow down before him, he is slow to relinquish the reins of office. Possession is nine points of the law. It requires a stern parent to make good the tenth. If the child no longer cries or has to be kissed, he makes up for it in other ways. He has breathed the free air of Australian independence too early to have much regard for the fifth commandment. To make himself a nuisance till he gets what he wants is the art he first learns and to this end he considers all means legitimate. Strict and *a fortiori* severe measures towards children are at a discount in Australia, and, considering the surrounding circumstances, by no other means can they be rendered tractable. The child has no restrictions put on his superabundant animal spirits, and he runs wild in the most extraordinary, and often to elders, unpleasant freaks. Certes the second stage is but little less unpleasant than the first,

When it gets into petticoats or breeches, the child must be treated of according to sex. And here *place aux demoiselles*, for from this time upwards they are a decided improvement upon their brothers. The Australian schoolgirl, with all her free-and-easy manner, and what the Misses Prunes and Prisms would call want of maidenly reserve, could teach your bread-and-butter miss a good many things which would be to her advantage. It is true that neither schoolmistresses nor governesses could often pass a Cambridge examination, nor have they any very great desire for intellectual improvement. But the colonial girl is sharper at picking up what her mistress does know than the English one, and she has more of the boy's emulation. Whatever her station in life, she is bound to strum the piano; but in no country is a good pianoforte player more rare, or do you hear greater trash strummed in a drawing-room. Languages and the other accomplishments are either neglected or slurred over; but, on the other hand, nearly every colonial girl learns something of household work, and can cook some sort of a dinner, yea, and often cut out and make herself a dress. She is handy with her fingers, frank, but by no means necessarily fast in manner, good-natured and fond of every species of fun. If her accomplishments are not many, she sets little value on those she possesses, and never feels the want of, or wastes a regret, on any others.

Almost all girls go to school, but the home-training leads to little obedience or respect for their teachers, and the parental authority is constantly interposed to prevent well-deserved punishments. Accustomed to form judgments early and fearlessly, each girl measures her mistress by her own standard; and if she comes up to that standard, an *entente cordiale* is established, the basis whereof is the equality which each feels to subsist independent of their temporary relations.

At seventeen my lady comes out, though for the last two, if not three or four, years she has been attending grown-up dances at the houses of friends, so that the edge of her pleasure has long been dulled. School once left behind, she looks upon marriage as the end and object of life; but it must not be supposed from this that she makes any attempt to catch a husband. Young men are plentiful enough, and she does not care when her turn comes. That it is bound to come she takes for granted, and accordingly is always on the look-out for it. The camaraderie which exists between her and some half-a-dozen men may lead to something with one of them; and meanwhile she has time to ascertain their dispositions and turn their qualities over and over in her mind till some one's attentions become marked, and she makes up her mind that she is suited or the reverse. She has danced too much before she came out to care much for it now; but in a warm climate, where verandas and gardens lend themselves so readily to flirtation, she retains a due appreciation of balls and parties, and gets a far larger number of them than an English girl of the middle class.

On the average, colonial girls possess more than their share of good looks; but 'beauties' are rare, and the sun plays the deuce with complexions. The commonest type is the jolly girl who, though she has large hands and feet, no features and no figure, yet has a taking little face, which makes you say: 'By Jove, she is not half bad-looking!' Brunettes are, of course, in the majority; and every third or fourth girl has beautiful brown eyes and an abundance of coarsish hair--which, by the way, she probably dresses in an untidy knob, all corners and no rotundity.

Her manners have lost the boisterousness of school days, but still often want toning down according to English ideas. Her frankness and good-fellowship are captivating, and you feel that all her faults spring from the head, and not from the heart. She is rarely affected, and is singularly free from 'notions,' though by no means wanting in ideas and in conversation of a not particularly cultured description. With a keen idea of the value of money and the benefits to be derived from its possession, she never takes it into consideration in choosing her husband: her ideal of whom is above all things 'manly'--the type that used to be known under the description of 'muscular Christians.'

In religion her views are not pronounced. She attends church pretty regularly, but is entirely free from superstition, though not always from intolerance. Adoration of the priesthood is not at all in her line. For politics she cares nothing, except in Victoria where naturally she espouses her father's side warmly, but in an irrational, almost stupid, way. Art is a dead letter to her, and so is literature, unless an unceasing and untiring devotion to three-volume novels be counted under that head. To music, according to her lights, she professes, and often feels, a strong leaning.

There is one thing about her that strikes you disagreeably in society. It is her want of conversation with ladies and married people. To a bachelor, to whom she has just been introduced, she will chatter away nineteen to the dozen; but, even in her own, house, she has no idea of the social duties. Marriage, in her opinion, is a Rubicon, which, once crossed, if it does not altogether debar from the pleasures of maiden and bachelorhood, at least makes it necessary for married folk to shift for themselves. To talk or dance with a married man would be a terrible waste of time; and as for married women, she expects to join that holy army of martyrs in the course of time, and will then be quite contented with the same treatment as she has meted out to others. The politeness which springs from a sense of duty to others is little known to the Australian girl. If she likes you, she will make herself very pleasant; but if you are not worth wasting powder and shot on, you must expect to realize that disagreeable truth in all its nakedness.

In many things a child, she often looks forward to her wedding for the mere festivity of the occasion, and thinks how jolly it will be to have six bridesmaids, how nice she will look in her bridal dress, and how the other fellows will envy her chosen one. Generally marrying two or three years younger than the English girl, she would consider herself an 'old maid' at twenty-three; and for old maids she entertains the very minimum of respect, in spite of their rarity in the colonies. Once married, she gives up to a large extent, if not entirely, the pomps and vanities of which she has had her full during spinsterhood, and devotes herself to her household, children, and husband. She usually has a large family, and in them pays for all the sins of her youth. She has had her fling, and for the rest of her life she lives but to serve her children and make them happy, recognising that in the antipodes 'juniores priores' is the adopted motto.

The Australian schoolboy is indeed a 'caution.' With all the worst qualities of the English boy, he has but few of his redeeming points. His impudence verges on impertinence, and his total want of respect for everybody and everything passes all European understanding. His father and mother he considers good sort of folk, whom he will not go out of his way to displease; his schoolmaster often becomes, *ipso facto*, his worst enemy, in the never-ceasing, war with whom all is fair, and obedience but the last resource. Able to ride almost as soon as he can walk, he is fond of all athletic sports; but it is not till leaving school that his athleticism becomes fully pronounced: thus reversing the order observed in England, where the great majority of the boys, who are cricket and football mad at school, more or less drop those pursuits as young men. He is too well fed and supplied with pocket-money ever to feel the need for theft, but it is difficult to get him to understand Dr. Arnold's views about lying and honour. Though not wanting in pluck, he lacks the wholesome experience of a few good lickings, and can easily pass his school-days without having a single fight. He is quarrelsome enough, but his quarrels rarely go farther than hard words and spiteful remarks. At learning he is apt, having the spirit of rivalry pretty strong in him.

In all but one or two schools classes are too much mixed to make a gentlemanly tone possible, and such little refinements as tidiness of dress are out of the question. When he is at home for the holidays, his mother tries to dig some manners into him (if she has any herself); but he has far too great a sense of the superiority of the rising generation to pay more attention to her than is exacted by the fear of punishment. Unfortunately, that punishment is very sparingly made use of; and when it is used, it takes a very lenient shape, public opinion being strongly against corporal punishment, however mild, and according to children a number of liberties undreamed of in the old country.

Indoors the Australian boy is more objectionable than the English one, because he is under less restraint, and knows no precincts forbidden to him. Generally intelligent and observant, he is here, there, and everywhere; nothing escapes him, nothing is sacred to him. Of course his further development draws its form and shape from his previous caterpillar condition, and when he comes to take his place in mercantile or professional life, he is equally disagreeable and irrepressible.

But such a young 'gum-sucker' must not be confounded with the ordinary middle-class Englishmen who form the majority of the professional and business men one comes in contact with in the present day. The native Australian element is still altogether in the minority in everyday life, and the majority of adults are English-born colonists. What modification then, you will ask, does the middle-class Englishman undergo in Australia? In some ways, a deterioration; in others, an amelioration. The deteriorating tendency shows itself in an increased love of dram--and especially spirit--drinking; in apparel and general carelessness; in a roughening of manner and an increase of selfishness. The improvement lies chiefly in greater independence of manner and thought, in a greater amount of thought, in enlarged and more tolerant views, in less reserve and *morgue*, in additional kindness of heart, and in a more complete realization of the great fact of human brotherhood.

In Australia a man feels himself an unit in the community, a somebody; in England he is one amongst twenty-seven millions, a nobody. This feeling brings with it a greater sense of self-respect and responsibility. Altogether, then, it may be said that the balance of the modification is generally on the side of improvement rather than of deterioration. The Englishman in Australia improves more than he deteriorates. And this is the more true the lower you descend in the social scale. It may be doubted whether the really well-educated man--the 'gentleman' in short, to use the word in its technical sense of a man well born, well bred, and well educated--generally improves in the colonies. As a rule, I should say he deteriorates. He cannot often find a sufficiently large number of his equals within a sufficiently small area, nor keep sufficiently amongst them not to lose somewhat in manner and culture. He develops the breadth, as distinct from the depth, of his intellect. He learns a great deal which he did not know before from the life around him, but he also forgets a great deal which he has learnt.

The great tendency of Australian life is democratic, i.e. levelling. The lower middle-class and the upper middle-class are much less distinct than at home, and come more freely and frequently, indeed continually, into contact with each other. This is excellent for the former, but not so good for the latter. In the generation that is growing up, the levelling process is going much further. The small tradesmen's sons are going into professions, and the professional men's sons into trades. You have the same tendency in England, but not nearly to the same extent.

Slight as is the division between the middle-class and the wealthy class, I ought perhaps to say a few words on the latter. Practically, as well as theoretically, there is no aristocracy in Australia, and the number of leisured men is yet too small for them to form a class by themselves. Still every day their number is increasing; and although they almost all do a certain amount of work, it is rather because, if they did not, they would find time lie heavy on their hands, than because there is any particular need for it. The wealthy squatter--which low-sounding word has in Australia become synonymous with aristocrat--spends the greater part of the year in supervising his station, although generally employing a manager, whose work bears much the same relation to his own, as that of the permanent head of a department does to that of his political chief. Whenever there is a race meeting or any other attraction, the squatter comes down (*not* up as in England) to town and spends a few days or a few weeks there, as the case may be. If he is a married man he probably keeps a town house, where his wife lives the greater part of the winter, which is the 'season;' if a bachelor, he lives at his club, which supplies him with lodging as well as board.

But he finds it hard work to spend any lengthened period in town. The clubs are deserted for the greater part of the day; everyone else has his or her work to do, and a lounger becomes equally a nuisance to himself and to his friends. With no tastes for literature or art, and little opportunity for their gratification if he should chance to possess them, he is thrown utterly on his own resources, and these rarely extend beyond drinking and gambling. Both these pursuits are more fitted for gaslight than daylight, and if indulged in too freely during the day, pall in the evening, so that he has literally nothing to do from breakfast till dinner. He cannot race or play cricket quotidianally, so that he soon returns to his station, where he stops till the next race meeting.

The wealth of Australia has not yet passed beyond the first generation. The majority of the wealthy have themselves made their fortunes, and are not inclined to let them be squandered by their sons, at least during, their lifetime. The number of young men with no regular employment is at present very small. And it is well it should be so. Else we should feel all the evils of a plutocracy, purified neither by education nor public opinion--evils which have already made themselves apparent in the political system of Victoria.

The Australian aristocrat has the greatest contempt for politics, and thereby has forged a collar for his own neck. The 'Berry blight,' as it is called, which has fallen over Victoria, is, to a great extent, a reaction against the selfish and inconsiderate policy of the squatters when they were in power. In such a crisis the mob has no time to be just, remembering only that the aristocracy were never generous. Politically, I fancy that the squatters will never again obtain power, except under conditions which will make a return to the old *régime* impossible. Socially, there are yet evil days before Australia.

There is a great deal of truth in the old saying--that it takes three generations to make a gentleman and there is no doubt but that the second is infinitely the worst of the three. Shortly the country will pass through a period when an unearned increment will fall into the hands of a half-educated class, whose life has nurtured in them strong animal passions; but I see no reason why we should not pass through the social as we are passing through the political crisis, and obtain a modified aristocracy in the third generation, which in the fourth should become as profitable to the country as an aristocracy well can be.

At present the old squatter drinks and gambles; his son will drink less, gamble more--though it was not a young man who recently lost £40,000 in a night's sitting at a club in Melbourne--and lead a wanton life; but he will probably have the sense to educate his children thoroughly, instead of taking them away from school at seventeen, as was done with himself; and the grandson will obtain some cultivated tastes which will make a fight for it with those he has inherited. In the fourth generation there should be an aristocracy, with as much similarity of character and disposition to the existing English aristocracy as the different circumstances of the two countries will permit.

The life of a wealthy woman in Australia is *ennuyeux* to a degree. If she is a lady by birth and education, she must necessarily feel that the advantages which wealth bestows are squandered upon such provincialism as she is perforce subjected to. To reign in hell is, after all, a very low ideal, and one which can only be entertained by an inferior nature, so long as heaven remains within reach. There are, of course, advantages in being rich even in Australia; but the wealthy lady will naturally draw comparisons between these and those which the same amount of money would procure for her in London or Paris. She can import dresses from Worth's, and carriages from Peters', but she cannot choose them for herself; and if they should be really admirable, who is there to appreciate their superiority to the surrounding fashions?

'How on earth am I to get on in Adelaide,' said a musician of considerable merit to me, 'when, as you know, there is no one with whom I can provoke comparisons?' The very superiority of the man was fatal to his success. And so it is with the Australian lady of taste. Nor does the misfortune stop there. Unless she makes frequent visits to centres of taste, I will defy any woman to retain her appreciation of good taste. Her own taste gets dulled by the want of means of comparison. You will perhaps say that taste in her surroundings is not everything which wealth can bring to a woman. But if you come to reflect for a moment, you will see that in the more comprehensive meaning of the phrase it is. Dress is but one example of the surroundings which a woman covets. I have chosen it because it is perhaps the commonest, though of course not by a long way the highest,

But wealthy ladies 'to the manner born' are not so numerous in Australia that I need dwell long on the drawbacks of their position. It is at any rate happier than that of the *parvenue*, unless the mere fact of being *arrivée* confers any special enjoyment. At what has she arrived? At carriages, at dresses, at houses and furniture, and at servants of a style she is totally unaccustomed to and unfitted for. When you tremble before your butler, and have to learn how to behave at table from your housekeeper, wealth cannot be unalloyed pleasure. Without education and taste, the *parvenue* has small means of enjoying herself except by making a display which costs her even more anxiety and trouble than it does money. Wiser is the rich woman who contents herself with the same style of life as she was accustomed to in her youth, adding to it only the things that she really wants--a more roomy house, a couple of women-servants, and a buggy. Thus she can feel really comfortable and at home; but unfortunately for their own and their husbands 'peace of mind' these poor women are too often ambitious to become what they are not. Even leaving aside the discomforts which are always allied to pretentiousness, the poor rich woman has a hard time of it. What can she do with herself all day long? She has not gone through that long education up to doing nothing which enables English ladies of means to pass their time without positive boredom. She has no tastes except those which she does not dare to gratify, and becomes a slave to the very wealth whose badge she loves to flaunt.

The Australian working-man is perhaps too well paid to suit us poor folks who are dependent upon him; but, for all that, comfortable means bring an improvement in the man as well as in his condition. It is very trying to have--as I recently had--to go to four plumbers before I could get one to do a small job for me, and still more trying to find the fourth man fail me after he had promised to come. Such accidents are of everyday occurrence in colonial life, and they make one doubt the advantages of a wealthy working-class. But, independent and difficult to please as the colonial working-man is, his carelessness is only a natural consequence of the value set on his labour. Provided he does not drink, you can get as good a day's work out of him as at home. He will pick his time as to when he will do your job, and hesitate whether he will do it at all; but having once started on it, he generally does his best for you. Too often the sudden increase of wages is too much for his mental equilibrium, and a man who was sober enough as a poor man at home, finds no better use for his loose cash than to put it into the public-house till. But as a class I do not think Australian working men are less sober than those at home. Those who are industrious and careful in a very few years rise to be masters and employers of labour, and are at all times so sure of constant employment that it is no wonder they do not care about undertaking odd jobs. If their manner is as independent as their character, I am far from blaming them for it, though occasionally one could wish they did not confound civility and servility as being equally degrading to the free and independent elector. But when you meet the man on equal terms in an omnibus or on other neutral ground, this cause of complaint is removed. Where he is sure of his equality he makes no attempt to assert it, and the treatment he receives from many *parvenu* employers is no doubt largely the cause of intrusive assertion of equality towards employers in general. Politically he is led by the nose, but this is hardly astonishing, since, in nine cases out of ten, his electoral qualifications are a novelty to him. He carries his politics in his pocket, or what the penny papers tell him are his pockets; or, if he rises above selfish considerations he is taken in by the bunkum of his self-styled friends. But in what country are the free and independent electors wiser? Happily for Australia, his Radicalism rarely lasts long, if he is worth his salt. He becomes in a few years one of the propertied class, has leisure to learn something of the conditions under which property is best preserved and added to, and thus--according to the admission of the leading Radical paper--Conservatism is constantly encroaching on the ranks of Liberalism. Except under very rare circumstances poverty in Australia may fairly be considered a reproach. Every man has it in his power to earn a comfortable living; and if after he has been some time in the colonies the working-man does not become one of the capitalists his organs inveigh against, he has only himself to blame.

Of the three sections into which the working-class may be divided--old chums, new chums, and colonials--the first-named are, on the whole, the best. For the most part they began life with a superabundance of animal spirits, and a love of adventure, which have been toned down by a practical experience of the hardships they dreamed of. They certainly drink most and swear most of the three sections, but with all their failings there are few men who can do a harder day's work than they. Barring pure misfortune, there is always some good reason for their still remaining in the class they sprang from. Though this is not always strictly true, since a good many of them began life higher up in the world than they are now. Still I prefer them to the pepper-and-salt mixture which has been sent out under that happy-go-lucky process--free immigration. When the colonies were so badly in want of population, they could not stop to pick and choose. Hence a large influx of loafers, men who, without any positive vice, will do anything rather than a hard day's work, and who come out under the impression that gold is to be picked up in the streets of Melbourne. Under the name of 'the unemployed' they are a constant source of worry to the Government, whom they consider bound to give them something light and easy, with 7s. 6d. or 8s. a day, and give rise abroad to the utterly false impression that there am times when it is hard for an industrious man to get work in Australia. Of course many of our immigrants have become first-rate workmen, but such men soon rise in the social scale.

The best workman when he chooses, and the most difficult to get hold of, is the thoroughbred colonial. Being able to read and write does not, however, keep him from being as brutal as Coupeau, and, except from a muscular point of view, he is often by no means a promising specimen of colonization. It is from this section of the community that the 'larrikins,' as they are called, are recruited, roughs of the worst description, insulting and often robbing people in Melbourne itself, and moving about in gangs with whose united force the police is powerless to cope. Sometimes they break into hotels and have 'free drinks' all round, maltreating the landlord if he protests. In a younger stage they content themselves with frightening helpless women, and kicking every Chinaman they meet. On all sides it is acknowledged that the larrikin element is daily increasing, and has already reached, especially in Melbourne, proportions which make it threaten to amount to a social clanger within a few years. Of late their outbreaks have not been confined to night-work, but take place in open daylight, *coram populo et* police. No one exactly knows how to meet the difficulty, and What shall we do with our larrikins?' is likely to replace the former popular cry of 'What shall we do with our boys?' to which some ingenious person furnished the obvious answer, 'Marry them to our girls.' Corporal punishment for corporal offences is in my opinion and that of most of the serious portion of the community, the only remedy which is likely also to act as a preventive; but however desirable it may be acknowledged to be, there is a difficulty in bringing it into use in communities whose sympathies are so essentially democratic as those of Victoria and New South Wales--for in Adelaide the police has still the upper hand. The votes of these very larrikins turn the scale at elections. Their kith and kin form a majority of the population, and therefore of the electorate. However much a member of Parliament or a Minister may recognise the necessity of meeting a social danger, he can hardly afford to do it at the expense of his seat.

At the time of the Kelly trial practical demonstration of the latent sympathy with crime in Melbourne was afforded. Thousands of persons, headed by the Chairman of Committees of the House of Assembly, actually agitated for the reprieve of the most notorious, if not the greatest, criminal in the annals of Australia, a man whose murders were not to be counted on the fingers; and all this because for over two years he had set the police at defiance, and after a life of murder and rapine had, shown the courage of despair when his only choice was between being shot by a policeman or hung on the gallows. In many respects, as, I have elsewhere intimated, our free political system makes the social outlook here far more promising than in Europe; but larrikinism is a peculiar danger already well above the horizon, against which we seem powerless to deal. Some set it down to the absence of religious teaching in the State schools, but its real point and origin seems rather to lie in the absence of parental authority at home and the unpopularity of the old proverb: 'Spare the rod and spoil the child.'

SOCIAL RELATIONS.

My last letter was necessarily, from the nature of its subject, a little flaky--a charge to which all these notes must more or less plead guilty. Though the heading of this one differs slightly, it must practically be a continuation of the same subject.

The first social relation, like charity, begins in the family circle, and was incidentally touched upon in my last. Between husband and wife the relations in Australia are, on the whole, probably as satisfactory as in any other part of the world. Both generally marry from love, and whatever may be the general effect of love-matches, it cannot be denied that more than any others they tend to promote pleasant relations between the 'two contracting parties,' as the French would call them. Amongst the wealthy, as everywhere else, there cannot of course be the close marital intimacy of the middle classes; but not only is infidelity less common than in London, but moreover, the proportion of the wealthy who keep up the style which produces the quasi-separation of domestic life is far smaller. Husband and wife have grown rich together; they have taken counsel together, and lived an open life, as far as each other are concerned, ever since they were married. Against this the usages of society, dressing-rooms and lady's-maids are of little avail. You may chase the second nature out by the door, but it jumps in again at the window.

In the middle and lower class the comparatively cribbed, cabined, and confined existence is also of the greatest service to that community of thought and action upon which conjugal happiness to so large an extent depends. Domestic occupations also occupy the thoughts of the wives, and business those of the husbands, so continually, as to leave few moments of mental vacuity for Satan to introduce mischief into. Of an evening the clubs are almost deserted, and their few occupants are nearly all bachelors, or married men who have left their wives in the country, having come down to town themselves on business. Drink must be recognised as a factor on the opposite side, and a by no means unimportant one; but there are many women who have no objection to their husbands drinking, so long as they either drink at home or come straight thither from the public-house.

I wish I could give as favourable a view of the parental relations. They are undeniably the weak point of family life in the colonies. During childhood a certain obedience is of course enforced; but public feeling is strong in favour of the naughty boy and wilful girl, looking as it does upon these qualities as prophetic of future enterprise. So many of our best colonists, it must be remembered, were eminently wild in their younger days, that it is no wonder they think 'there is something' in the self-willed child. Their own life has been too much of a struggle for them to be able to appreciate at their true value the gentler qualities which in themselves would have been of little worth, the victory in their earlier days having been to the physical rather than to the intellectual. The child is naturally--for surely disobedience is an 'original sin' with nine children out of ten--only too disposed to take advantage of the views held by its parents, and gradually as it grows older, disobedience passes into disrespect and want of respect into want of affection. Such a thing as perfect confidence, in the French sense of the word, between a parent and his or her grown-up child is most rare. 'Everyone for himself, and devil take the hindmost, is the motto of the young Australian. He cares for nobody, and nobody need care for him, so far as his thoughts on the subject are concerned. Maternal affection cannot, however, be easily quenched, and consequently the child gets all the best of the bargain.

Social relations are wider, therefore less easy to speak about decidedly, than family relations. In the early days there were but few social distinctions. Everyone was hail-fellow-well-met with everyone else, and the common struggle merged all differences of birth, wealth, and education. In a charming little work called 'Some Social Aspects of South Australian Life,' which was published in Adelaide about two years ago', a most realistic description is given of the sympathetic mode of living of the first settlers; and as it has never been reprinted in England, I extract a few sentences here and there, which may give some idea of the primitive existence there described:

'The necessaries of life were produced in abundance, the comforts were slowly reached, and the luxuries had to be done without. There was very little difference in the actual circumstances of different classes--some had property and some had none' (this was before the gold-fever); 'but property was unsaleable for money, and barter only exchanged one unsaleable article for another' (and yet these are the people who nowadays groan about *money* going out of the colony, and would measure its prosperity by the excess of exports over imports).* [* The parentheses are my own.] 'Nobody employed hired labour who could possibly do the work himself, and everyone had to turn his or her hand to a great deal of miscellaneous work, most of which would be called menial and degrading in an old community. . . Thus gradually the financial position of the colony improved by means of the well-directed industry of the settlers, and they owed much to the helpfulness and good management of the wives, sisters, and daughters of each household. . . Perhaps, never in any human society did circumstances realize the ideas of the community of labour and the equality of the sexes, so fully as in South Australia in its early days.' Youth and love, hope and trust, were the only stock in marriage of young couples, so that a new-comer is said to have remarked, 'Why, it is nothing to get married here! A few mats, and cane-bottomed chairs, and the house is furnished.' A wife was not looked on as a hindrance or an expense, but as a help and a comfort,' says Miss Spence.

'Girls did not look for establishments; parents did not press for settlements . . . There was only one carriage in the colony for many years, which though belonging to a private person, was hired for such as wanted to do the thing genteelly . . . .' Social position depended on character, and not on income.

The same writer lays herself fairly open to the charge of being *laudator temporis acti* in her description of the present as compared with the past social life of the colonies, though I am quite prepared to agree with her remark, that 'in proportion as the conditions of life become more complex, they should be met by more ingenuity, more culture, and a deeper sense of duty;' and that 'the suddenness of our accumulation of wealth has scarcely prepared our little community for some necessary modifications of our social arrangements.' Therein lies the whole source of both what is best and what is worst in the present social life of Australia. Marriage, though still almost entirely an affair of love, has yet learnt to take £. s. d. into consideration, and none but the lowest class would be satisfied with the kind of furniture described above. Education has improved and is improving still more, far as it yet is from being up even to the English standard. More leisure has also produced novel reading with its consequent affectation of aristocratic ideas and prejudices and disproportionate estimate of essentials and superficials.

Already each Australian capital has its 'society,' distinguished from the [Greek characters] almost as clearly as in London or Paris. In its own way, indeed, these societies are more exclusive than those of the older metropolises, which from their very size obtain a certain breadth of view. For obvious reasons the component parts are not altogether similar, but their governing idea is as much the same as the difference of circumstances will permit. It would be difficult to define exactly what opens the doors of Australian society, but is the shibboleth any more definite in London? Distinction of some kind or other must be presupposed. If that of birth, it must either be allied to rank or have strong local connections. Is it not the same in London, though, of course, on an infinitely larger and grander scale? If that of wealth, it must storm the entrance by social expenditure and pachydermatousness to rebuff. Wealth is, of course, the predominating factor here, as rank in London; because while in the latter case birth calls in wealth to furnish it with the sinews of war, in the former wealth calls in birth to teach it how to behave itself. Position is of small account, though the line is always drawn at shopkeepers *in esse*. Provided the candidate has cut the shop and opened an office, he can be admitted on payment of the social fees, but only gradually and laboriously unless his wealth is beyond criticism. The man who sells you a dozen of wine in the morning sits by your side at Government House or Bishop's Court in the evening, and the highest officials are not unfrequently the least esteemed socially. A happy consequence of this social jumble is, that with certain exceptions, which are, of course, getting more numerous as we advance in civilization, a gentleman can do anything here and still be considered a gentleman, provided he behaves himself as such; and the semi-menial employments of distressed gentlewomen do not bring with them one half the loss of social position that they generally entail in England. The smaller community is more narrow-minded than the large, but its sight is keener and more accurate in details. It is true that art, science, and literature are entirely without status in Australia, but then personal distinction of whatever kind is far more get-at-able than at home.

If it strikes a visitor as utterly ridiculous that a society, the greater part of whose members are essentially *parvenus*, should assume the tone and mode of thought of an old-world aristocracy, we must yet acknowledge that that society keeps up a great many traditions of refinement which are in great danger of being lost sight of in colonial life. The outward and visible sign may be absurd, but the inward and spiritual grace is none the less concealed within it. That Australian society keeps up a number of social superstitions which might with advantage have died out during the journey across the ocean is undeniable, but it is also true that it preserves at least an affectation of higher civilization. It contains the majority of the gentlemen and ladies by birth and education in each city, and they go far to leaven the whole lump. The *parvenu* has the merit of seeking after better things, and his imitation of aristocracy, if it necessarily falls far short of the mark, at least removes him a step or two above the way of thinking common to the class he sprang from. His daughters, with that superior adaptability inherent in women, are quick to catch the manners of the gentlewomen who move in their circle, and become infinitely superior to their brothers, even when the latter have been sent to finish their education at Oxford, or Cambridge. It is wonderful how much more easily a lady can be manufactured than a gentleman.

Of the hospitality of 'society' in all the towns it is impossible to speak in too high terms. The stranger has but to bring a couple of good introductions to people who are in society, and provided he be at all presentable, the doors of the most exclusive houses will be opened to him. Young men of education and manners are everywhere at a premium, and the colonies are still small enough for it to be a distinction to have just come out from England. Unless you know your company it is always wise to avoid asking questions about or making reference to the earlier days of the people you meet. For all that, you will hear everybody's history, often, I suspect, with additions and exaggerations. In such small communities everybody knows everything about everybody else, and the man who has gone down in the world naturally delights in telling you of the time when he bought half a pound of sugar at Jones's shop, or when Brown worked in his garden while Mrs. Brown was his scullery-maid, Jones and Brown being now two social leaders.

Amongst men social distinctions are very slight. It is lawful to be friendly with everybody and anybody in town, so long as you do not visit at his private house. And yet for very obvious reasons gentlemen are--except amongst the rising generation--much more common than ladies. A number of wild young men of good family and education have been poured out of England into Australia ever since 1852, and many of them have become amongst the most useful and respected colonists. But until recently there was a paucity of ladies, and the majority of gentlemen had but the choice between marrying beneath them or not at all. Hence frequent *mésalliances*. You meet a man at the club, and are delighted with him in every way. He asks you to his house, and you find that his wife drops her h's, eats peas with her knife, and errs in various little ways. I am purposely thinking of no one in particular, but fear at least a dozen of my acquaintances will think I am writing of them in making this remark. And it is a sad sight to see a man dragged down in this way, for very few men who marry beneath them can keep up the manner and mode of living to which they were born and educated, while those who do generally retain them at the expense of their own married happiness. Nowadays there are certainly plenty of young ladies in the towns, but for all that one constantly hears of the sons of clergymen and army officers marrying the daughters of grocers and farmers who were quite recently day-labourers. With every freedom from caste prejudice, I am yet unable to see anything but harm to the persons directly concerned in these ill-assorted matches, whatever the good result to the community may be.

The centre round which society revolves is naturally Government House, but a great many people go to Government House who cannot be considered to be in society. To have been to a Government House ball is no more, *mutandis mutatis*, than to go to a Court ball at home. Neither will give you admission into the inner circle; and though that circle may not offer any but specious advantages and have but little to recommend it in preference to three or four other societies in the town, admission into it is coveted, and inclusion within its boundaries is as much a reality as if its walls were of stone. In Melbourne the scattered position of the suburbs and the extent of the population splits up the *élite* into several local societies, but there is yet one *crème de la crème*. In Sydney the same thing takes place, though the local societies are less numerous; but in Adelaide there is practically only one 'society', the local aggregations of individuals not being deserving of any more dignified name than 'cliques.' Of the three societies, that of Sydney is on the whole, I think, the best. At Melbourne there are probably a larger number of cultivated persons, but the distance between the suburbs and the more extravagant mode of living limits their sphere. The Adelaidians are perhaps the most English of all in their way of thinking, but they are also by far the most narrow-minded. For pure Philistinism I don't think I know any town that equals it. Shut up in their own little corner, they imagine themselves more select than Sydney and Melbourne circles, because they are necessarily smaller. And yet for kind-heartedness these gossip-loving Philistines are not easily to be surpassed. As long as things go well with you they will talk against you; but no set of people are less open to the charge of neglecting friends in misfortune.

Class relations are, on the whole, excellent; and this is the more to the credit of the lower classes, because the plutocracy is utterly selfish in character, and does not interest itself in those social duties, which are proving so effectual a prop to the nobility and landed gentry of England. A certain animosity subsists between the squatters or pastoral lessees and the selectors who purchase on credit from Government blocks of land, which were formerly let to squatters. At times this breaks out in Parliament or at elections, but in spite of a determined attempt by a section of the Victorian press to pit the 'wealthy lower orders' against the horny-handed sons of the soil, class feeling rarely runs high for any length of time. The reason is, that the working-class are too well off for the occasional high-handed proceedings of the rich to affect them sensibly. For an agitation to be maintained there must be a real grievance at the bottom of it; and the only grievance that the Australian democrat can bring forward is, that having obtained the necessaries, he cannot without extra labour obtain also the luxuries of life.

From figures I have already given as to rents, wages, and prices in general, you will have gathered that the cost of living is, broadly speaking, cheaper than in England as regards the necessities of existence, but dearer in proportion to the complexity of the article. Anything that requires much labour, or that cannot readily be produced in the colony, is, dearer; but, on the other hand, it should be remembered that money is more easily obtainable. Protectionist duties and heavy freights form an effectual sumptuary tax; and as most of the duties are *ad valorem*, first-class articles are heavily handicapped, and a premium put upon the importation of shoddy. The wine-drinker finds that he has to pay ten shillings a gallon on all he drinks, which should certainly entice him to drink good wine; but the only practical result discoverable is the small quantity of wine drunk as compared with beer and spirits. If few people keep carriages, there are buggies innumerable in every town; and for every man who keeps a horse in England, there are, proportionately to the population, ten in Australia.

But perhaps the greatest element in the cheapness of colonial life is its comparative want of 'gentility.' The necessity to keep up appearances is not one-sixth as strong as in England. The earthen pot cannot altogether flow down stream in company with the tin kettle, but it can more safely get within a shorter distance of its metallic rival. Rich men live in miserable houses and wear coats which their valets would have nothing to do with at home; struggling men are less ashamed of struggling, and are not made to feel the defects of their condition so keenly. In a society, the position of whose members is constantly changing, the style of life is of less importance. The millionaire of to-day hadn't a sixpence yesterday, and may not have one again to-morrow. His brothers, sifters and cousins are impecunious, and in small communities poor relations are not easily got rid of. Constant intercommunication is thus kept up between class and class, rich and poor; they learn better to understand each other's position, and a clearer understanding generally leads to mutual respect.

Again, the distribution of wealth is far more equal. To begin with, there is no poor class in the colonies. Comfortable incomes are in the majority, millionaires few and far between. This is especially the case in Adelaide, where the condition of the poorer class is better, and that of the richer worse than in any of the other colonies. In Melbourne the masses seem worst off, and the display of riches, if not the actuality thereof, is most noticeable. In Sydney the signs of wealth are not wanting to an examiner, but a superficial observer would say that there were not half as many wealthy men as in Melbourne. Few South Australians get beyond the comfortable stage, and, on the other hand, a greater number reach it. 'Squatting,' of course, supplies the largest section of the wealthy class; but, especially in Melbourne, gold-mining and commerce have contributed a large quota.

RELIGION AND MORALS.

In no country in the world is the legal freedom of conscience more firmly established than in Australia. All Churches and sects are absolutely equal in the eyes of the State; and any attempt to upset this equality would be resented, not only by the united forces of all the other denominations, but even by a majority of the only two Churches--the Roman and Anglican--who would ever dream of aiming at supremacy. But thorough as is the repudiation by the great majority of the community of the principles of State aid or control of religion, the two Churches which I have just mentioned occasionally raise their voices against secular education by the State, and make spasmodic appeals for State contributions to their denominational schools, which, however little likely to succeed, are not altogether without a rational foundation. But this is the utmost limit which State recognition, or rather the cry for it, is ever likely to reach.

In times past the Church of England has struggled to regain the position she formerly held in the older colonies; but now whatever efforts she makes in that direction are confined to the ambition of being *prima inter pares*--a position which is vigorously and even bitterly attacked by the other Protestant sects whenever she either tries to assert it or has it thrust upon her. These ex-Dissenters have a lively remembrance of the yoke they endured in the old country, and even now that the spirit of supremacy has so completely died out, they spring up to do battle against any formality that recalls it to them. Thus, a few years ago the whole colony of South Australia was convulsed on the question of the Bishop's right to follow the Governor and precede the Chief Justice at official ceremonies, and peace amongst the devout was only restored by the Bishop's graceful relinquishment of a position to which his legal right was undeniable. Even now the title 'My Lord' as applied to Bishops acts as a red rag on many ex-Dissenting bulls, and they are as jealous of the slightest official preference of the Church of England as if their dearest religious liberties were therein involved.

Legal and even official equality do not, however, always mean social equality; and the Church still retains a superior social position, a shadow of her departed State authority, which to some of her old competitors--especially the Congregationalists, Baptists, and Wesleyans--is the more galling because they are totally destitute of the means of assailing it. Happily, through the wise conduct of the Bishops of Adelaide and Melbourne in meeting ministers of other denominations on a common platform, whenever the cause of Christianity or of good and right in any way can be served thereby, and in showing sympathy with them in a multitude of ways, this unreasonable jealousy is losing ground and a better feeling springing up; but there are yet too many colonists that have felt the disabilities of Dissent in the old country who are unable to put on the armour of forgiveness, or rather of forgetfulness in the new. The enemy has lost his sting, but they will not allow him to live on the remembrance of his past greatness without a reminder of his present impotence.

This impotence is in all ways, except socially, a certain reality; for while the ex-Dissenting bodies have thriven and waxed numerous and powerful upon the bread of independence, the Church has languished for want of her accustomed prop. Accustomed, not only to support their own ministers, but also to pay tithes and Church-rates for the benefit of their rival, the ex-Dissenters have simultaneously had their burden lightened and, for the most part, their incomes increased by the change of country. Besides this, they have to a certain extent felt themselves put upon their mettle to show their superiority to their old master, and thus they have put their best foot foremost, with the good result which always attends such efforts. Their ministers, better paid, and holding a higher social position than in England, have naturally become a superior class of men as a whole to those in the old country. Every day they are advancing, towards a higher standard of education and manners. Nor has the gain in education and position been accompanied by, as far as I can see, any loss in earnestness or deterioration in work. No one sect is sufficiently preponderant to admit of that.

The friendly competition between them has been beneficial to them all; and, in spite of rivalry, the spirit of toleration between Protestant sects is thoroughly observed. Unfortunately, this toleration is not extended to the Roman Catholics. Their doctrines are so directly in opposition to the prevailing democratic and Protestant spirit of the community, that they have come to be regarded as Ishmaelites, if not as Amalekites, occupying ground which ought to belong to the faithful. An Anti-Popery cry would at any time command success; and numerous and influential as the Catholics are, directly they begin to assert their influence all the other religious bodies unite to counteract, and end by suppressing it. For a spice of intolerance in this respect, and for a general Philistinism in its views on all subjects, Australia is indebted to the middle-class Protestant sects, who form the most important element in the community; but to them also, in a large measure, it owes its political and social stability, and all those standard moral qualities which are the only safe foundation for a superstructure of intellect.

Because I have spoken so warmly of the good influence which the ex-Dissenting or Protestant sects have exercised in Australia, it must not be supposed that the Church has been altogether a laggard. Probably no section of the English clergy has worked harder and more manfully than that which has been stationed in Australia. It is no fault of theirs if their sphere has been limited and their good influence less effective than that of their rivals. But they have been labouring under the misfortune of being unsuited to the people and circumstances amongst whom and which they live and work. Their sphere has lain almost entirely amongst the upper and lower classes, and it is neither of these that governs Australia. Where they came into contact with the middle class, the power in the land, they have been placed in the position of the round man in the square hole. The men of the middle class have asserted their social equality to, if not their superiority over, their clergy; and this an English gentleman finds difficulty in admitting, still more one who considers himself the minister of God to the people, rather than of the people to God. The Thirty-nine Articles do not admit of his recognising the orders of his nonconformist brethren as equal to his own, and this has been set down to pride. Altogether, the Anglican clergyman has been put in a false position, to extricate him from which is taxing all the tact of so politic a prelate as Bishop Moorhouse.

The habit of paying no direct stipend to their clergymen in England has led to a reluctance to contribute good salaries for their support out here, where they must rely solely upon such support; and the lowness of salaries, if not the hardness of the work, has made the Anglican clergy in Australia as a class inferior to their English brethren. Of course the clergy still contains a large proportion of gentlemen within its ranks, but on the score of ability I fancy the ex-Dissenters have the advantage. Recognising this, Bishop Moorhouse is endeavouring both to shame Churchmen into raising the stipend of their clergy, and to procure for the congregations not only English gentlemen, but as far as possible hard-working, practical, broad-minded men. He has a difficult task before him, for already there are plenty of colonial clergymen who are either inferior to nonconformist ministers in cultivation, or stubborn adherents to a *régime* which is impossible in Australia. These weeds must be pulled out before you can sow fresh seed; and yet it is hard to call men weeds who are serving the Church according to the best of their lights, faithful, hard-working men, or conservative old gentlemen, who are doing or have done a great deal of good work, and whose failings cannot be attributed to any fault for which you can morally reproach them.

The Church is slow to adapt itself to colonial life. Amongst a preponderating lower middle-class element Nonconformity, or rather what is better known as Protestantism, is very popular. Low Churchmen find they can get a better sermon at the chapel, and can be hail-fellow-well-met with their pastor in these extraneous denominations. Thus the Church loses many of its former adherents, and while Anglicanism still remains the religion of the upper class, it can in no way pretend to be that of even a majority of the community.

The Roman Catholics are on a different footing. For them no compromise is possible, and they cannot as Roman Catholics but be a state within a state. From time to time the priesthood incites them to aspire to political power, but hitherto none of these aspirations have borne practical effect, except in strengthening the hands of their adversaries. At present they are agitating more or less vehemently in each colony for State support to be given to their schools, declaring that it is monstrous that they should be made to pay for a secular education of which their religion prevents them from taking advantage.

At first a section of the Anglican party, comprising nearly all the clergy, joined in this cry, but it became so evident that the bulk of the population was determined not to return to the old system, that they are beginning to desert the Catholics, and are now more wisely and with better chance of success attempting to amalgamate with the other Protestant bodies to obtain the admission into the State schools of religious teaching on a broad Protestant basis; i.e., of all the doctrines which are held in common by all Protestant denominations (except the Unitarians), to the exclusion of all doctrines on which the different sects differ. The bulk of the Dissenters are, I fancy, indifferent to any junction with the Church of England, and would just as soon have no religious teaching as what they call a 'pithless jelly-fish' religious teaching. But on this point I think public opinion is undergoing a change, and the formation of a Protestant party probable. The Catholics would consider such a concession as infinitely worse than the existing purely secular system. The omission of true doctrine would, as regards them, amount to an assertion of false; and on their side in opposing the Protestant party will be the Jews, the Freethinkers, and a large number who would rather have no religious teaching than any quarrel over it, and who are fairly satisfied with the existing state of things. If the Protestants ever become strong enough to win the day, it can only be at the expense of establishing a Catholic grievance so strong as to be exceedingly dangerous. The fact that all parties are now out in the cold, satisfies a rough-and-ready conception of justice with which the politician has always to reckon, but that all the Protestants should get a concession, of which it is impossible for the Catholics to avail themselves, would be manifestly unfair. Political expediency and justice seem to be alike against the claims of the Protestant party, unless it be resolved to grant aid to Roman Catholics and Jews only, which is a possible, though not very consistent, solution of the question.

Ritualism is unknown, though the word is often applied to the one or two High-Church services in the capitals where the choirs wear surplices, or, worse still, where there are candles on the altar--a word which is almost as much objected to as priest. Broad and Low are decidedly the prevailing phases of Churchmanship, and every year the Broad is gaining upon the Low; the Low element consisting of those who were brought up in England, the Broad of the generation which has been born in the country. As this begins to predominate, the barriers between the Anglican Church and the other Protestant denominations will be lowered, and in course of time the differences between them will be reduced to preference in the mode of conducting service. The first step towards this was taken by the Bishop of Melbourne some two years ago in forming the Pastoral Aid Society, the object of which is to provide religious services in outlying districts in the bush, where there are not sufficient settlers of either the Episcopalian or Presbyterian Churches to make it possible to supply a minister of either. The Society arranges that services should be held in these districts alternately, according to the rites of each Church, and that they should be visited alternately by ministers of each.

This system has proved of enormous value in keeping religion alive in the bush, and paved the way for an experiment not long ago in Melbourne itself, which has met with such general approval, that it may be said to mark the commencement of a new era in the Church of England, and even in ecclesiastical history. With the consent of the Bishop and of his church-wardens, Canon Bromby invited a Presbyterian minister--Rev. Chaos. Strong-to read the service and preach in St. Paul's Church, he himself taking Mr. Strong's pulpit. This precedent is certain to be largely followed; and it is easy to see that the courtesy which is extended to Presbyterian ministers will before long be extended to those of the other Protestant denominations, and that exchanges of pulpits between them all will become frequent.

Churches abound in every Australian city, especially in Adelaide, where they are so numerous as to excite the ridicule of the less devout Victorians. I forget how many there are; but, at any rate, they bear a very small proportion to the public-houses, against which I think they may fairly be pitted. Still, there are plenty of them; and no sinner will easily be able to find an excuse for not going to church in the non-representation of his particular sect. When I say 'churches,' I am using the term in the official and colonial sense, for the word 'chapel' stinks in the nostrils of a Dissenting community, and many of these churches are not much bigger than an ordinary dining-room, and, having been built for profane purposes, have no external odour of sanctity beyond a black board, whereon you are informed, in gilt letters, that the building belongs to whatever sect it does belong, and that Divine Service is held there by the Rev. So-and-So at certain hours on the Sabbath. But from this you must not suppose that the two older churches have a monopoly of the religious buildings which can properly aspire to that name.

For the most part, ecclesiastical architecture is rather a weak point with these newly-confirmed religions; but in Melbourne, with the exception of the Roman Catholic Cathedral, they possess far the finest churches, and in Adelaide and Sydney their edifices are at least imposing. The Roman Catholics., however, carry off the palm. In both Melbourne and Sydney their cathedrals are of grand proportions. In all three cities their other churches are large and lofty. The Anglicans have small cathedrals at Sydney and

Adelaide; but, in spite of their including a majority of the wealthiest individuals in the colonies, they find a great difficulty in raising money for building purposes.

As far as my experience goes--and I have 'sat under' the principal ministers of each denomination in each town at least once--the preaching is, for the most part, very poor. There are certainly two or three exceptions; but 'what are they,' one is irreverently apt to exclaim, 'among so many?' The shallowness and often halting pace of these discourses is doubtless due, in large measure, to the colonial love of *extempore* preaching. For sermons read out of a book public opinion of all denominations in Australia has the greatest contempt. Like English lower middle-class communities, again, they like a good pronounced type of doctrine from the pulpit. The lower regions are popular; but most successful is the denunciation of the people over the way who bow down to wood and stone, and commit sundry other iniquities for which Protestants are in no fear of being indicted.

As you notice a man's general appearance and manner before you can form any idea of his character, so I have described churches and denominations before entering seriously into the question of religion. If Churchmen--who will probably form the majority of my readers--cannot but be grieved at the picture I have drawn, of the condition of the Australian Church, they may at least take comfort when I state that the preponderating feeling of Australian cities is essentially Christian, according to the received meaning of the word. The citizens are, for the most part, of a distinctly religious turn of mind. They may not be, and--except in Adelaide--are not, such good church-goers as at home; but they have not drunk of the poison of infidelity, nor eaten of the sweets of indifference. Amidst the distractions of colonial life this could hardly have been the case, but for the Puritan origin of so many of the more influential among them, and the healthy competition between the various sects, as well as the freedom from State control and interference already alluded to.

As in social matters Melbourne may be regarded as the extreme type of Australia, so in religious matters Adelaide affords the easiest text to preach upon. Essentially lower middle-class, Nonconformist and Radical in its origin, South Australia might well claim the title of the New England of the Antipodes. Even to the present day, it preserves signs and tokens of the Principles on which it was founded: its progress having been the gradual and healthy growth of a Pastoral and agricultural colony, undisturbed by the forced marches of gold-mining. In Adelaide middle-class respectability is too strong for larrikinism, and imparts a far healthier social and moral tone than obtains in either Melbourne or Sydney; but for these advantages the little town pays the small but disagreeable price of Philistinism. Want of culture, Pharisees, and narrow-mindedness find a more congenial home there than anywhere else in Australia; but, to my mind, these are a cheap price to pay for the piety and real goodness which they cloak.

The Adelaidian may be unpleasantly conceited and self-satisfied in religious matters, but then he is kind and hospitable, religious and moral, and not so sophisticated as the Victorian, who is probably a more agreeable person superficially. Yet in neither Melbourne nor Sydney can religion be said to be wanting. It is kept more in the background than in Adelaide, and there is not so much of it as in the smaller town; but the religious character of all three, taken either singly or together, will, I think, compare favourably with that of any other modern city or cities.

Sabbatarianism is fast on the decline. The Sabbatarians are still noisy and determined enough to keep the majority of our public libraries, picture galleries, etc., closed on Sunday, but this is more from public indifference on the subject than from any general feeling that they ought to be shut. This becomes evident from a visit to the suburbs on a fine Sunday. All the world and his wife in private carriages and buggies, carts and omnibuses, even on Shanks's pony, come away for an airing; and if the weather only allows of it, there are many of these holiday-makers who make a day of it, leaving their homes early in the morning, with but a few who return to evening service.

On the other hand, the Sunday is soberly kept. In the less strict families music is allowed, but never cards or games of any kind. The man who proposed such a thing in Adelaide would be *anathema maranatha*. The general feeling, is, that the Sunday was made too wearisome in England to be supportable in a common-sense community; and Sabbatarianism is gradually losing ground day by day, as fast as the keeping up of appearances will allow. There was a great outcry on one occasion because the Governor of Victoria travelled on a Sunday; but this was rather because there is a general feeling that unnecessary labour should as far as possible be avoided on a Sunday, than from Sabbatarianism in the ordinary sense of the word.

Morality has so long been connected with religion that it is difficult to treat of the one without more or less trenching upon the province of the other. But there still remains something to be said on this score. The commandments which are most freely broken in Australia, are *par excellence* the third, and then the sixth, in its minor sense of crimes of violence in general. Young Australia makes a specialty of swearing. High and low, rich and poor, indulge themselves in bad language luxuriantly; but it is amongst the rising generation that it reaches its acme. The lower-class colonial swears as naturally as he talks. He doesn't mean anything by it in particular; nor is it really an evil outward and visible sign of the spiritual grace within him. On the prevalence of larrikinism I wrote at length in a former epistle.

Drunkenness comes next on our list of vices. That Australians as a nation are more drunken than Englishmen, I do not believe to be the fact; but what is undeniable is, that there is a great deal of drunkenness amongst those who may claim to be considered the upper classes here. An English gentleman of the present day, whatever his other sins may be, does not get drunk, because it is 'bad form,' if for no better reason. If in Australia we were to exclude as 'outsiders' all the leading colonists who are in the habit of intoxicating themselves--to say nothing of the chance customers--'society' would dwindle down to nearly two-thirds its present size. But there has been a very appreciable improvement in this respect during the last half-dozen years, and the tone of public feeling on the subject is gradually approximating to that of English society. The old colonists are not of course expected to change their habits in their old age, but with the young generation there is less tippling, and port, sherry, and spirits are being replaced by claret.

Of drinking as apart from drunkenness I have already said enough. The seventh commandment is one of those unpleasant subjects which one must deal with, and which one would yet prefer to leave alone. Generally speaking, one may say, that while our upper and lower classes are, if anything, rather worse in their morals than in England, we make up for the deficiency by a decided superiority amongst the middle--both upper-middle and lower-middle--class. Conversation is perhaps coarser here; but whatever may be the reality, the moral standard generally accepted is superior to that of London. Such immorality as exists is necessarily of a coarser and more brutal type. In Melbourne, especially, the social sin is very obtrusive. Sydney has of late been acquiring an unenviable notoriety for capital offences, and it is not advisable for ladies to walk alone in the streets there at any time of the day. On the other hand, in Adelaide no woman who does not give occasion for it need ever fear that she will be accosted.

Larrikinism is certainly a troublesome phase to deal with; but burglaries are exceedingly rare, and it may fairly be said, that life and property are more secure in the Australian capitals than in any European towns of the same size. As in all large cities, the scum or dregs of the population gradually localizes itself, and thus becomes easier of control, even though it may increase in amount. And here, Adelaide has an advantage in being seven miles distant from its seaport, which naturally retains a large portion of the noxious element. Melbourne has two disadvantages, which tend to make it the sink of Australia--firstly in its metropolitan character and central position, and secondly in the admission of a large number of bad characters at the time of the gold-diggings. Sydney, of course, retains traces of the old convict element--an element, however, which must be acknowledged to have contributed to the good as well as to the bad qualities which are peculiar to New South Wales.

EDUCATION.

That very profound saying about the victory of the German schoolmaster has not been without effect even in this distant land. During the last decade education has been the question *du jour* here; not that we have studied it physiologically and psychologically and culture-logically, as you have been doing in England. Theologies are a little beyond our ken, and we leave it to the old country to discover, by a harmonious combination of deductive and inductive teachings, what education really is. Our educational crisis has been merely legislative and administrative; but it is no small transformation for us to have emerged from the chrysalis state of clerical and private-venture instruction into the full butterflydom of a free, compulsory and secular national system. And that not before it was time. Whatever may be the demerits of uniformity, State-interference, secularity, etc., etc., it does not leave room for the same incompetence in teaching and ignorance on the part of the learner, as frequently occurred in the old happy-go-lucky fashion of schooling. Australian children have all now the chance of learning the three R's according to the latest and most approved fashion, and if their parents choose they can also get a smattering of history, geography, and one or two other things into the bargain.

The history of our educational evolution is perhaps worth summarizing. In the early days of colonization the Church of England spun an educational cobweb, which it has been very difficult to sweep away, and which still remains in a fragmentary state as an evidence of past good service. When the education of the first settlers was in danger of being altogether neglected, the Church put forth the greatest energy to meet their wants, raising funds both here and at home to provide schools and teachers. The Catholics, and later on other denominations, followed her example; and thus, at a time when the State was fully occupied with attending to more primary wants, an education was provided which, considering the circumstances and viewed according to the lights of those days, was highly creditable. The State subsidized these schools, as well as others which were established by private venture in townships where no denomination was sufficiently powerful to establish a school at its own cost. Boards were appointed to control the subsidies and roughly estimate the teaching of each school, and in New South Wales these boards had also power to establish national as opposed to denominational schools wherever opportunity offered. You can easily imagine how inefficient and extravagant this subsidizing arrangement proved. In small townships where a single State school could have given a good education to all the children in the district, there arose two or three denominational schools, all drawing money from the public purse, and yet each too poor and too small to teach well. At last in 1873 Victoria led the way in discarding the denominational schools, and starting at enormous expense an official system of free, compulsory, and secular primary instruction throughout the colony.

In 1876 South Australia followed suit, though in that colony the schooling is only free to those who cannot afford to pay a fee of fourpence per week for children under seven, and sixpence for older children. Finally in 1880 New South Wales also threw off the yoke, which she had only borne longer than her neighbours because her old system was far superior to theirs. Here, too, a weekly fee of threepence per child is demanded, but no family may pay more than a shilling per week, however large in number, and in cases of inability the fees are remitted.

All three Education Acts agree in their main bearings, though differing considerably on points of detail. The system of district and local boards of advice is largely made use of in all of them, but the compulsory clauses have never been properly enforced, principally on account of the great difficulty of doing so in thinly populated districts. The word 'secular' admits of different variations in each province. In Victoria moral truths form the limit. In New South Wales an hour a day is set apart for religious instruction from the mouth of a clergyman or other religious teacher, if the parents do not object. In South Australia Bible reading is permissible, but comment on the text forbidden. It is yet too early to pass a definite judgment on the new systems, but it is already evident that the teaching in the State schools is much better than in those denominational schools which survive. Vigorous efforts are still being made by the Roman Catholic Church, with some aid from the Anglicans, if not to upset the new schools, which has become impossible, at least to regain a subsidy for their own, but, I fancy, with less and less chance of success every year, in spite of the fact that in Victoria the agitation is at present especially strong. The fact is, that while a large number of people agree that purely secular education is to be deplored, no feasible scheme can be propounded for introducing religious instruction into the State schools which will satisfy the demands of the Catholics. The Protestant denominations might without difficulty agree upon a common platform, and it is on the cards that they may, in spite of the Catholic opposition, succeed in introducing a modicum of religious instruction into the State schools. The Catholics maintain that false religious teaching is worse than no religious teaching, and will be satisfied with nothing less than a subsidy to their own schools.

In spite of the yearly immigration of a number of children too old to learn to read and write in Australia, statistics show that in 1878, out of 100 boys and girls between the ages of 15 and 21, no less than 93 could read and write--a result which must be considered creditable to the old 'arrangements.' But what the statistics cannot show is the meaning of that phrase 'read and write.' It is in quality far more than in quantity that the teaching of the State schools is superior. To my thinking, one of the best superficial proofs of their success is the number of middle-class children who are sent to them even in the towns. Previously these children had often grown to be nine or ten years old without schooling or teaching of any kind, and even now much of the time of the secondary schools is wasted in teaching simple primary subjects, which ought to have been at the boy's fingers-ends before he came to them.

With the exception of an experimental higher school for girls, recently established at Adelaide, the State in Victoria and South Australia takes no part in providing secondary education. In New South Wales it has begun to do so, but as yet only on a very limited scale. To meet the wants of the colonists in this respect, two classes of schools have been established: denominational and private venture. The first class have often got good foundations, and taken as a whole they may be compared to the middle-class schools, which have recently been established in several parts of England, the two or three best rising decidedly above the level of the best of these, but not being able to reach that of English public schools even of the second class. Nor in spite of the vigorous efforts that are being made in some quarters will a public school tone ever be possible in Australia, so long as the majority of the boys attending are day-boarders. In all day-schools the authority of the head-master is necessarily impaired by that of the father, and the discipline of the school by that of the home; but here this is more than usually the case. The parents even go so far as to trench upon the schoolmaster's domain, reserving to themselves the right of deliberately breaking the school rules, whenever it is convenient to them to do so. 'Some parents,' writes the head-master of what is probably the nearest approach to a public school in Australia, 'keep their boys from school for insufficient reasons, and without leave previously obtained, to carry a parcel, or to drive a horse, to have hair cut, or to cash a cheque, or simply for a holiday.' Being an old English public-school boy and master, and fresh to colonial ways, he writes thus in his report for 1875; but in the report for 1880 he has to acknowledge that he cannot maintain the rule he had introduced, that no boy should be absent from school except on account of ill-health or stress of weather or after obtaining the leave of the head-master,'because I have not received adequate support.' 'The school cannot, single-handed,' he continues, 'press the point, if parents do not like it. The strain upon me, individually, is too great, if I have to remonstrate with a parent, or to punish a boy, on an average about twice a week.' The boys cannot be got to come back to the school on a certain day, or prevented from leaving before the term is over, many parents being of opinion that little is done the first week, and that therefore they may as well keep their sons at home.

How hard this is for the schoolmaster who has his heart in his work, it is easy to see; and I was quoting an instance where a man of great resolution and perseverance had made an attempt under circumstances perhaps more favourable than could be obtained in any other school in Australia; for the school was certainly the best in the colonies from a social standpoint, and very nearly so intellectually at the time he took it. He himself, too, was summoned from England with the avowed purpose of introducing the public-school system. In no other Australian school would a five-years struggle of this kind be possible. Nor would this be a solitary instance, for though naturally one cannot gather it from published reports, the whole existence of a schoolmaster in Australia, who wishes to do his duty, and understands what that duty is, must be, on many important points of discipline and sometimes even of teaching, one continual struggle with the parents. In too many schools the parent not only uphold their boys in direct disobedience to their masters, but even encourage them in it out of personal dislike to them. In a small community, the master who dares kick against the parental goads soon finds the town too hot to hold him. He has but one choice, either to sail with the parental wind, or to lower his canvas altogether; and though a man of tact may make some progress by trawling and tacking, at the best he must feel disappointed at heart and his interest in his work half gone.

Turning to the schools themselves. The divergence is so considerable, that any remarks I make can have but a very general application. At the best, the social tone is better than at your middle-class schools; at the worst--I am still only speaking of grammar schools and denominational colleges, the highest class of secondary schools--it is no worse; while the moral tone never falls to so low a level, and in some cases almost rises to that of second-rate public schools at home. The Church of England grammar schools are naturally the best in social tone, the boys being drawn from a better class of parents; and I am by no means sure that the morals and manners of boys do not, to a certain extent, go together. In the special sense of the word 'morality,' the best colonial schools can, I think, challenge comparison with your, public ones; but the regard for truth needs strengthening. On the other hand, theft is almost unknown. The same master from whose reports I quoted above, tells me that he finds colonial boys quite as tractable and amenable to discipline as English, when the authority over them is paramount; but in most schools this is far from being the case, the fault often, no doubt, lying with the master's want of tact. I still have a lively remembrance of the difficulty I had in keeping discipline on an occasion when I helped to examine a well-known college; but then, even at the best English public schools, the upper forms have a disposition to 'try it on' when a new hand is set over them, as my own reminiscences tell me.

In the Victorian Schools, and in secondary, as in higher education, Victoria offers infinitely superior advantages to those of the other colonies combined.

A feeling of *esprit de corps* exists; not so strong, perhaps, as in English public schools, but very strong considering the number of day-boys. In the other colonies it does not take root at all firmly, or else degenerates into party spirit -a tendency which it also shows in Victoria, where it is moulded into better form by the masters. In most schools the prefect system has been established, of course with large modifications. It has difficulties to struggle against in the democratic spirit of the country, and in the early age at which the majority of boys leave school; but in its working shape it seems to do good. This is especially the case at one or two Victorian colleges, where the masters have established a mutual feeling of trust between themselves and the boys; but at too many the natural opposition remains. The masters get too easily disgusted at what they consider the rough manners and ways of the boys, and are contented to leave them to their own devices, so long as they get through their work and obey the rules. Consequently the boys become rougher and less amenable. Another difficulty in the path of good discipline and tone throughout the schools is the too advanced age at which boys come there.

One of the greatest difficulties a head-master has to contend with is, that there are practically no preparatory schools, even in Victoria, to feed the large ones; and often, through a sudden rise of his parents' circumstances, or from some other reason, a boy is sent to school for the first time, at fifteen or sixteen, knowing nothing beyond the three R's. Others are taken away in the midst of school-work, either to go to Europe with their parents, or because times are bad, and then brought back after a couple of years with formed habits of idleness and independence which it is difficult to subdue. Looking at the last report of the Melbourne Grammar School, I find the average age of the upper sixth to be 17 1/2 of the first form 13 1/3; but I fancy that at the majority of schools the averages would be quite a year younger in both forms.

At schools, as at home, more liberty has to be conceded to Australian than to English boys, and the circumstances of their life make them more fitted for it. But masters complain that parents of day-boarders do not take enough trouble to see that their boys work, and leave them too much choice of studies. This latter defect results from the strong feeling in favour of individuality amongst colonists, which leads them to favour the idea of each boy from the first striking out a line for himself, without considering how far he is a competent authority as to his own capabilities. Where parents do not interfere, obedience to rules is generally well enforced and that, although punishments are much lighter than in England, and the cane is only brought into use for extreme offences. The staff of masters is usually fairly strong as regards ability and attainments, but, as is too often the case in England, the majority of them are neither trained teachers, nor even with an aptitude for teaching; they have simply taken to this particular profession because they could get more immediate return from it than from any other. The headmasters, or rather those of recent appointment, are, as a rule, well chosen. Their salaries run from £800 to £1,200 a year; and you can get either a first-class man, whose health prevents him from remaining in England, or a good second-rater for that sum. In some schools the council or permanent board of governors work excellently with the headmasters; but too often the Australian dislike to absolute authority in whatever shape or form is so great as to induce the council to become meddlesome; and unduly interfere with the master.

So much for the constitution of the school. The work though also modelled after the English system, diverges from it considerably to suit local requirements. English public-school training is directed to lead up to University teaching; thereby losing in amplitude and finish, but gaining in density and stability of groundwork. But here, although the majority of boys matriculate, they do not go to the University; and, to suit them, the University has itself been forced to widen its basis. It has become, to a large extent, an examining body for a kind of *Abenturienten* certificate, and of necessity the matriculation examination which serves this purpose has had to extend over a wider area. These two circumstances, reacting the one upon the other, have kept the school-teaching wide, whereby, of course, it loses something in depth. Thus the master of a leading school complains of the little time that is given to classics--only less than a quarter of the total school-hours to Latin, and no more to Greek, which is, moreover, an optional subject.

But before you begin to blame our system--which, I may prophesy, will soon have to be adopted in England--you must remember the central fact that nine Australian boys out of ten finish their education when they leave school, i.e. at sixteen or seventeen. Four of the nine go into business, three into the bush, and the other two directly into professions. Obviously the interests of the nine are of far more importance than those of the one, and it is for their benefit that the system of education must be arranged. As the country advances in civilization, we may reduce the proportion of those who have to face the world directly they leave school to 80 or even to 75 per cent.; but even then it is only possible to consider the interests of the minority to a certain extent. I will grant that that extent should be greater than the numerical proportion, because the aim of a school must keep a certain elevation if it intends to keep above the average of schools; but it is impossible to make a silk purse out of a sow's ear, and the *main* bearings of the school must reflect the purpose for which the majority of boys come there, if it is to be of any service, or to achieve any legitimate success.

For my own part, I am not altogether inclined to regret the little attention that is paid to Latin and Greek. Mr. Matthew Arnold's complaint of half-culture has always seemed to me to savour of the pedagogue, and his school of the prig--though I use these words in the better shade of their meaning. It would, I believe, be a gain if the splitting of the educational system into denominational schools had not taken place. A school with 200 boys--the usual size of our largest--cannot give the twofold training, classical and modern, side by side, as most of your public schools are doing now; but I am not sure that what the classical side gains by such a division, is not lost by the modern side as compared with the homogeneous system.

School-work nowadays cannot be mere training and foundation-laying. It would be absurd to expect it to cover every department of the higher education, but there is a happy mean discoverable between the two. A compromise can be established by which, while a preference is given to such studies as science and mathematics, which may be held to represent the inductive and deductive training, boys may yet carry away from school a reasonable amount of practical knowledge, which, if they do not allow it to get altogether rusty, can be of use to them in its direct application to their after-life, as well as in its indirect influence. To meet some such views as these, the heads of our best schools are allowing considerable latitude of subjects in their upper classes; but in most cases it would probably be better for the man if the boy's future career, being once settled, and his own and his parents' tastes consulted, the decision as to what optional subjects he should pursue were left with the head-master, the parent, of course, retaining a right of veto.

But I am lapsing into an educational dissertation, and must hasten back to colonial school-work. Leaving out of consideration exceptionally clever boys, the average of learning at our better grammar schools is higher than in middle-class ones, which form the fairest standard of comparison obtainable, but lower than at public schools. The four or five top boys in the upper sixth would invariably be in the sixth at Harrow or Rugby: at times eight or ten would. The rest of the upper sixth would probably be well up in the upper fifth, or in what at Rugby is called the 'Twenty,' while the lower sixth would compare with the lower half of the upper fifth, and higher half of the middle fifth. Here I am taking as our standard our three or four best schools, all of which, except the Sydney Grammar School, are Victorian. The two South Australian colleges and other leading New South Wales establishments fall far below this standard.

I think I alluded before to the want of preparation for secondary education, and the interruption of the age-equality of the schools by the advent of boys of fifteen and sixteen, who have to be put in the first or second form Between them, these two causes lower the age-standard so much that one must, on the average, estimate that a colonial boy is two years behind an English one in point of education. This is most visible at the beginning of school-life, where, as you will have noted, the first form averages over thirteen years old, but is partially made up by the superior rate of progress if the boy remains long enough. At seventeen he should not be more than a year behind his English contemporary.

The setting up of the matriculation examination as a standard up to which the average boy strives to make his way, has undoubtedly had a beneficial effect. Being a reachable proximate ideal, it works strongly upon every boy's *amour propre*, egging on the average and lazy to work, and by a system of honours holding out hopes of distinction to the able. The practice of giving text-books for it encourages cram, and its width allows of shallowness; but, to counteract this, distinction in any particular subject is very highly marked.

That there should be a disposition here to look coldly upon the old-fashioned classical education is not wonderful. You are beginning to have your doubts about its superiority even in England. Here the majority of parents would just as soon bury the past, and everyone who becomes a *bonâ fide* Australian must feel that the history of his country is yet only in embryo. Besides this, the tendency of a new country is towards practical knowledge--small profits, and quick returns; and in classics the outlay of time is considerable, the returns slow, and the profit not always very perceptible. Science receives daily increasing attention, as at home. Geography is better realized by colonial children, and, I should fancy, better taught. In fact, all English subjects, as they are called, get their fair share. Mathematics, even in those lower branches which come within the scope of a school, are not a favourite subject, although about the same number of school-hours are devoted to them as at home.

The school-hours generally begin about nine a.m.; but school lasts till twelve. Second school begins at two, and lasts till four, when the day-boys go home. Half-holidays, ordinary or extraordinary, are rare; but Saturday is always a whole holiday. The main bulk of holidays are at Christmas, when some seven weeks are usually given. The midwinter vacation rarely lasts a month, and short breaks are allowed at Easter and Michaelmas, after the fashion of all schools comprising any large number of day-boys. As in England, the Easter term is the laziest; but here it is so for a good and sufficient reason--the heat during that period being often intolerable.

Nearly every Australian school has a stable attached, in which boys who ride to school put up their horses during school-hours. It is most amusing to watch half a dozen 'fellows' galloping their ponies up the avenue, not to be late for first school, just as we used to scurry across quad to chapel of a morning! The ordinary sleeping and living arrangements for boarders are much the same as at home. At the Sydney State Grammar School, which is in reality purely and simply a day-school, several of the masters take boarders, in imitation of public-school boarding-houses. At the Melbourne Grammar School the second-master has a house, the property of the school; but, so far, there are not more boarders than will fill the school-house.

The bill of fare of public schools has, I believe--thanks to scarlet fever and doctors--improved considerably since my day; but I do not suppose it has yet reached the luxury of unlimited meat and jam three times a day, with frequent bountiful supplies of fresh fruit. It is as necessary to the credit of an Australian school to keep a liberal table, as it is for an Atlantic steamship company. Where several schools are pretty well on an equality, the table often turns the scale.

In Victoria, especially, the boys are inordinately fond of games and outdoor sports of every kind; but too many of the day-boys prefer playing cricket and football with local clubs to joining in the school games, and this makes *esprit de corps* only possible between school and school. There are no divisions sufficiently strongly marked in the school to become parties. Sixth and school are perhaps the nearest approaches; but the day is far distant when intellectual differences will be appreciated by grown-up colonists, much more by schoolboys; and it is only in a few schools where a 'sixth' and 'school' match is possible. Untidiness in dress, and indeed in all of their belongings, is another of the colonial schoolboys' weaknesses. At the Melbourne Grammar School the boys have studies which they in a certain way appreciate; but they are quite content with the bare floor and walls, and would despise the little attempts at comfort and prettiness which an English boy makes. The latter's pride in his study would be quite incomprehensible to the colonial, who not unnaturally imbibes his ideas from the rough-and-ready mode of living in his home. As for uniformity in dress, he would be a bold master who would even attempt to carry it out.

What I have written of the grammar-schools and denominational colleges of course applies more or less to all secondary schools. There is at this moment near Melbourne a private-venture college, which, owing to the great ability and reputation of its head, ranks with the best Victorian grammar schools. I should doubt whether the tone that is possible in a non-proprietary school can easily be brought about in a private one, but in teaching power it is certainly not inferior. With this one exception, the private-venture colleges established in each suburb of the different capitals are little better than the commercial academies of England. There is the same bad tone, want of sufficient numbers of boys of equal standing in the school-work, and other disadvantages, which make the very name of a private school malodorous. The boys are rough and unmannerly, the discipline slack, the teaching staff inferior in ability and social position. The public schools of Australia may not be all that could be wished, but [Greek characters] that a boy of mine should ever go to a colonial private school, unless it were a preparatory school--a class of institution greatly needed and not yet provided, because parents do not appreciate the need.

The existence of three universities in a country with less than two million inhabitants speaks well for the colonists' appreciation of the higher instruction, which they themselves have rarely had the opportunity of enjoying. The Sydney University, founded in 1851, was the first in the field, but in spite of fine buildings, affiliated colleges, able professors, and a very fair supply of funds, it has never succeeded in attracting any considerable number of students, and can hardly be said to have won even a *succès d'estime*. No little of its failure is attributable to the success which has attended its Melbourne rival, founded in 1855, at the height of the gold-fever, and which may be said to have been floated on gold directly, and kept in deep water by it indirectly. Before Sydney could recover the effects of the emigration of those years, Melbourne was well under way, and the size and central situation of the latter city contributed no little to the success of its young university, which, under unusually politic as well as able management, increased annually in size and usefulness, until now no less than 1,500 students have graduated in its halls, and the number of undergraduates attending its lectures exceeds 280. It confers degrees in arts, laws, science, medicine, surgery, and engineering--the standard for which is above that of Oxford and Cambridge, and in medicine is higher than that of London itself. All the professors are men of first-rate ability. Amongst them are an F.R.S. (M. McCoy, Professor of Palaeontology), and Dr. Hearn, the well-known authority on jurisprudence and constitutional law. By acting as an examining body for the secondary schools, the university has not only widened its sphere of usefulness and materially raised the general educational standard of the colony, but has gained influence in circles, into which not even its name would probably otherwise have entered. Already a certain healthy tone and *esprit de corps* obtains amongst the students, and *ceteris paribus* a Melbourne graduate is professionally to be preferred to an Oxonian or Cantab., at any rate for colonial work. Thanks in no small degree to its educating and civilizing influence on the community, an anti-materialistic voice is beginning to make itself heard in Victoria, and if it does not occupy itself too much with politics, it promises to become an intellectual centre. It would not be difficult to find faults in either its constitution or its teaching, but it has the great merit of taking the trouble to understand and keep abreast of the times. All things considered, the Melbourne University may claim to have deserved the success it has commanded, and to be one of the greatest achievements of Victoria.

The present prosperity and bright prospects of New South Wales, together with the educational influence of the late exhibition, and an opportune bequest of £180,000 by a wealthy colonist, have lately stirred up the authorities of the Sydney University to make a grand effort to justify its existence. A medical school--*the* most successful side of the Melbourne 'varsity is to be established, and other improvements introduced. But although the principal, Dr. Badham, is a better classic than any that the Melbourne University possesses, there is an indolence and *laissez-faire* about the Sydney University which must long keep it in the background. Not until there is a thorough reformation in the whole style, tone, and management of the university will there be any real progress, and the centripetal influence of successful Melbourne is so strong, that I do not believe Sydney will ever be able to catch up lost ground, or even to considerably decrease the interval between itself and its rival, advance though it may, and undoubtedly will, when the present governing body has died out, and the public insists upon an entirely new regime. As for the Adelaide University, it is bound either to federate with Melbourne on the best terms it can obtain, or to drag on in extravagant grandeur. In five years of existence it has conferred five degrees at a cost of £50,000, and the professors threaten to outnumber the students. The vaulting ambition of the little colony has somewhat o'erleaped itself; but by a federation with Melbourne there would undoubtedly be practical benefit gained, and little but sham glory lost. If Sydney would also forego its jealousy, and acknowledge the success of its rival by federating on a basis which should allow the Melbourne University the position of *prima inter pares*, all colonies would profit; but even if Sydney would federate--which I do not think in the least probable--it could hardly expect its successful *confrère* to meet it on terms of perfect equality, especially as, comparatively speaking, Melbourne has little to gain by federation.

As regards the cost of secondary and higher education, it must be considered exceedingly small, remembering that the value of money is less here than at home; and that the salaries paid to masters are from £50 to £200 a year higher than the same men would obtain in England. The highest terms for boarders at any secondary school are £80 per annum, and from £50 to £60 is the usual charge. Day-boys pay from £12 to £24, according to the school. The University fees are very light, amounting to not more than £20 to £30 a year, including all charges.

As the Universities are purely teaching and examining bodies, with but little control outside their walls, the religious denominations are beginning to supply the want of a college system such as obtains at Oxford and Cambridge, by founding affiliated colleges in which the regime approximates as closely to that of the English Universities as the circumstances of the case allow. At Melbourne there are two of these colleges--Trinity College, belonging to the Church of England, and Ormond College, erected at the cost of some £70,000, and richly endowed by a wealthy colonist, Mr. Ormond, belonging to the Presbyterians. At Sydney, the Roman Catholics, the Church of England, and the Presbyterians, have all three erected affiliated colleges, but they are smaller and less successful than those at Melbourne, and in a large measure serve merely as theological colleges for training young men for the ministry. The Church of England in Adelaide has also founded St. Barnabas College, where, however, the relative importance of the two duties is reversed--the college being more especially a theological college. The Sydney colleges have not at all fulfilled the expectations which had been formed about them, largely owing to the want of success of the university; but the Melbourne colleges, and especially Trinity College, which is the least richly endowed, and has the smallest buildings, are doing excellent work. The atmosphere which the students breathe in them is conducive to greater steadiness of work and exertion to achieve university honours than is generally found in the unattached student; besides, they offer some social advantages, and are also morally tonic. In founding Trinity College, which was the first of these institutions in Victoria, four years ago, the Bishop of Melbourne may be said to have conferred an educational boon upon the colony only second to that which it owes to Sir Redmond Barry. Every year it is increasing in usefulness, and I can well understand that many parents who before preferred the expense of sending their sons to Oxford or Cambridge, will now see their way to allowing them to complete their education at the Melbourne University.

The provision for the secondary education of girls in Australia is miserably poor. The only school that really combines the social and intellectual qualifications requisite is to be found at Perth, in Western Australia. At that school the teaching is admirable and the social tone excellent. The only other school where girls are well taught is the High School at Adelaide, but being a day-school and a State-school, it cannot be expected to pay much attention to the social side of education. The private schools for girls attain but a poor standard in instruction, and a worse one still, when socially considered. There is one in Melbourne considerably superior to the rest; but if I had daughters of my own, I should certainly not send them to any as boarders, and would think twice before I sent them as 'day-girls', if the expression be allowable. But it is only fair to these schools to say that my standard of what a girls' school should be is very high. It is, however, satisfied by the Bishop's Ladies College at Perth.

POLITICS.

The chief interest of Australian politics lies in their relation to those of the Mother Country. Having imported their whole constitution and law books holus-bolus from England, each colony has been engaged ever since its foundation in fitting them to its circumstances. The legislative equipment of the young Australias corresponded pretty nearly to the tall hats and patent-leather boots which fond mothers provided for the aspiring colonists. An exogenous growth has prevented originality of ideas, which for the most part have been supplied by English thinkers, but the adaptability and less complicated social machinery of a young colony have permitted the carrying into execution of many valuable measures long before they emerged from the region of theory in their native land. It would not be hard to multiply instances where important reforms have been hastened and made practicable in England by their adoption and favourable operation out here, or avoided on account of their failure here. Australia is the *corpus vile* on which England makes her legislative experiments. In this direction there is a great deal of useful information in the study of our politics to an outsider; but to go into the question at large would take up a three-volume publication instead of a short letter, and my present purpose is merely to give an outline of the existing situation in each colony, only touching upon so much of their past history as is necessary for the understanding of their present position.

The most interesting, history is that of Victoria, the youngest colony of the three, which up to the time of the gold discoveries formed a district of New South Wales, not inaptly named by its first explorer 'Australia Felix.' Practically, its history may be said to date from these gold discoveries in 1851. For the next five years adventurers of all nations and classes flocked to the diggings, and quiet settlers from other colonies left their sheep to look after themselves while they hastened to reap a share of the golden harvest. Fortunately the diggings only gave place to mines which are still a staple of wealth. But during the period of the American war the gold tide ebbed too swiftly, leaving high and dry not only diggers, but the thousand-and-one classes who were indirectly dependent upon the gold supply. The better portion of these found occupation on the land--the richest in Australia, though neglected during the gold mania. But there remained a large number without any visible means of support, and not particularly inclined to go out of their way to find any. What to do with this large class of 'electors' became the question of the day, until in 1865 Sir James M'Culloch introduced a scheme for making work for them. By turning the tariff into an industrial incubator he forced manufactures into existence, and gave employment to those who had nothing better to do. It was in this manner, to meet a temporary crisis, and with no deliberate economical purpose, that the thin edge of the protectionist wedge was introduced. When once the purpose for which the duties had been imposed was served, the originators of protection in Victoria thought they could be quietly dropped. Needless to say, it was easier to call in the spirit of Protection than to lay it again. The gold produce continued to decrease, and the cry was for more duties and heavier duties, until a please-the-people Ministry extended the list to every possible article of manufacture, and raised the duty to a prohibitive amount-for many articles as high as $27\frac{1}{2}$ *ad valorem*. The colony has now committed itself to an almost irrevocable extent. Even the relative idea of imposing duties temporarily for the sake of giving new industries a start, which marked the second stage of public opinion, is giving way to the absolute one that Protection means more work and higher wages whenever and wherever introduced. It may in course of time be possible gradually to take 5 per cent off the duties at a time. But any reduction of the tariff would instantly put hundreds of electors--and very noisy hundreds too--out of employment, and reduce the earnings of thousands, while the general effect upon prices would take a long time to become perceptible. At the present time, come Conservative, come Liberal into office, neither's tenure would be worth twenty-four hours' purchase if he made any attempt in that direction. The whole subject of Free Trade and Protection has for the present completely passed out of the region of practical politics.

A distinguishing feature of Victorian public life is the existence of an approach to definite political parties bearing the same names and starting originally from the same bases as in England, though their principles by no means correspond to those of English Liberals and Conservatives. The main factor which led up to these divisions was class dislike, embittered by the remembrance that both plutocracy and democracy started in life on an equal footing. The diggings caused a general shaking up of the social bag, and the people who came out uppermost were mostly those who had been lowest before. In matters political they grabbed the public lands wholesale; socially they flaunted their wealth more openly than was wise. *Du haut en bas* came badly from those who had only a few years ago been hail-fellows-well-met. On the other side was jealousy, embittered often by a feeling that it was a man's own fault that he had not got on better in the world. The change had been brought about too suddenly to allow of people shaking down into their new positions. In this state of public feeling demagogues were not slow to see their advantage. They fanned the flames of discontent and jealousy till they broke out in Mr. Berry's 'platform,' the bursting-up of the landed estates, reform amounting to revolution, protection *ad absurdum*, and so forth.

For a short time feeling ran so high over the Reform Bill, as almost to threaten civil war. One minister talked of settling the question with 'broken heads and flaming houses.' Another boasted at a public meeting that he had 'got his hand upon the throat of capital'--all bombast, of course, but dangerous bombast at a time of great public excitement. Happily a vent was found for these angry passions in the ridiculous incident of Mr. Berry's 'embassy' to the Colonial Office, which set both parties laughing, and after three years of turmoil which had led to considerable commercial distress, everybody got tired of agitation.

The Berry Ministry died of ridicule. A Conservative Government then enjoyed a short tenure of office, but committed suicide by bringing in an impracticable Reform Bill. A second Berry Ministry came into office, but not into power. It also lived a few months, but with its dying kick it passed a measure which, though it placed the Upper Chamber on a more liberal basis than any other in Australia, and effected most important changes in its constitution, was conservative in comparison with Mr. Berry's first proposals. Hitherto members of the Upper House had been elected for ten years, the qualification for the electorate being the possession of property of the rateable value of £50 a year. Now the electoral qualification has been reduced to £10 house and £20 leaseholders, and the tenure is for six years. The Lower House, or Assembly, has for years been elected by manhood suffrage throughout Victoria, New South Wales, and South Australia.

Land reform has not yet advanced equally far, and will probably be reserved for the next burst of democratic energy. The view of 'the party' is that land should be made to pay a tax proportionate to the increase which the State has, directly and indirectly, effected in its value by railways and otherwise. The more advanced section point out that the greater part of the land was sold at ridiculously and dishonestly low prices to friends of the powers that were. For this reason, and because the wealth of the colony would, they contend, be increased in the gross, as well as more equally distributed by the partition of the large freeholds, the tax should be progressive, i.e. increasing in percentage according to the value of the property, so as to compel the large owners to sell, and establish something answering to a peasant proprietary, or, more strictly speaking, a yeomanry tilling its own soil. The Conservatives look upon such a tax as nothing better than legalized robbery, and hold the most pronounced views on the sacred rights of property. A *juste milieu* will probably be found between the two courses, and the existing land-tax be increased; but unless recent legislation for Ireland inspire new views of property, I do not think a progressive tax is to be feared. As regards the existing land laws, I shall say something further on upon this point in connection with those of New South Wales.

After a bout of rabid Radicalism, Victoria now owns, or is owned by, a half-and-half Ministry made up of the weakest members of both parties. Its views are Liberal-Conservative, and wishy-washy; its principal concern to remain in office. It serves as a sort of Aunt Sally for both parties to shy at. But there is no coalition strong enough to replace it. For nearly two years now it has pursued the even tenour of its way, harmless and unharmed, confessing where it has blundered, and dancing a sword-dance among small matters of administration. So long as it occupies itself with nothing of importance, it seems likely to remain in office till the next General Election. In view of this event, Sir Bryan O'Loghlen has introduced a four-million loan to provide fifty-nine railways, which should conciliate the hardest hearts of his opponents in every district; for these railways are to be distributed most impartially, and if any districts have more than a fair share, it is those where opposition is most likely to be met. Unfortunately for the Government, a series of accidents on the suburban railway lines have recently called public attention to the fact that political influence is more useful than competence in the obtaining of employment in the railway department. The O'Loghlen Government have not been greater sinners than their neighbours in this respect; but unless they take the bull by the horns, and speedily bring in a measure to hand over the management of the railways to a non-political board, they are likely to be sacrificed to public indignation. The failure of the loan will also be laid to their door and if either Liberals or Conservatives can only organize themselves sufficiently, the General Election will probably prove fatal to them.

Of all the Australian provinces, there is none with the immediate resources and future prospects of the Mother Colony. On her varied soils and amidst her different climates, wool, wheat, wine, and sugar all find a roomy and congenial home. Gold, copper, and tin are not wanting; and close to the seaboard she has an unbounded supply of coal, which must eventually be of more service in raising up manufacturing industries than all the protective tariffs of Victoria. The early circumstances of New South Wales were against its rapid growth. Founded as a receptacle for convicts, a system akin to slavery soon took root. Such of the early settlers as were neither gentlemen nor convicts belonged to the lowest class, or joined it soon after they landed. The colony was more than half a century old before it got any backbone; and although the descendants of convicts have in most cases proved excellent colonists, it took some time before 'trust in the people' could get the upper hand of fear. Even now, when but few of the last convicts remain above ground, and the masses of the population consist of immigrants in every way equal to the other colonies, the spirit of Conservatism is still ingrained in New South Wales. The shadow of the past still lingers behind in its comparative social and political stagnation, in an indolence and want of enterprise which is past all understanding to the Victorian, and a cherishing of prejudices long after they have been rooted out in the Sister Colonies. Even that arch-Democrat Sir Henry Parkes can only govern the colony by setting himself up as the reverse of Mr. Berry.

New South Wales is constantly claiming credit for its adoption of a Free Trade policy, but even this was brought about more by good luck than good management. The circumstances which gave birth to Protection in Victoria never occurred in Sydney. No one ever thought of such a thing. A light tariff, founded on no particular principle, had been levied for many years for revenue purposes; when, on the eve of a General Election, Sir Henry Parkes, on the look-out for a good safe, cry, brought forward, under the seductive form of 'remission of taxation,' the existing tariff, which, though it manages to bring in as large a revenue as the Victorian Protectionist one, limits considerably the number of articles taxed. This was the first strike-out in the direction of Free Trade. The subsequent buoyancy of the circumstances of the colony, and the applause with which nearly the whole Australian press greeted the plunge, have confirmed the policy, and made it a safe political watchword. But a great deal remains to be done before New South Wales adopts Free Trade as it is understood in England. From the outward and visible sign to the inward and spiritual grace, is often a far cry.

In New South Wales, as in Victoria, large tracts of land have been bought up at very low prices to form single estates. But the province is much larger than Victoria, and thus feels the loss less. It was here that the squattocracy was first successfully attacked. In 1861 Sir John Robertson passed an Act by which any person can select as much as 320 acres of Crown land in any part of the colony at the rate of £1 per acre, only 25 per cent. of which is payable on the spot, provided he subscribes to certain conditions of cultivation and of residence on his 'selection.' This Act was subsequently copied in Victoria, and is now being altered there so as to enlarge the area selectable to 640 acres. Although often leading to great injustice, this has certainly afforded a healthy outlet for democratic passion. The plutocracy of New South Wales have risen to wealth less rapidly than in Victoria, and have lived much more quietly and with little display. And thus it comes about that there is very little class feeling in the colony, and politics are carried on without any more dangerous outbursts than the personal conflicts of excitable members of Parliament.

Not only does party government not exist in New South Wales, but burning questions are few and far between. Since 1878 the lion has been lying down with the lamb, and the Parkes-Robertson Coalition Government has had to raise a powerless opposition to keep itself from death by inanition. Personal politics are always more or less the order of the day, and Ministers are well content that as much superfluous energy as possible should be spent on petty squabbles between private members, and on such local questions as the taking of railways through certain districts, or the building of police-courts in certain townships. Of course, when the General Election comes, they are bound to have something to swear by, and as they are not particularly troubled with either memory or conscience, they generally have no difficulty in sailing before the wind, even if they have to 'bout ship.

The late Premier, Sir Henry Parkes, has a special aptitude for discovering which way the wind is going to blow, which places him first on the list of living Australian politicians. Whilst colonists have appreciated the compliment paid to them in the flattering reception which he has recently met with in London, no one who has lived in Sydney can forbear a smile at the idea of Sir "Enery' passing as a representative of the respectable portion of the Australian community, to whom, for the most part, he is only less obnoxious than Mr. Berry.

The ink with which I wrote the last paragraph had not been dry a fortnight, when the unexpected news came of the defeat of the Parkes-Robertson Government on their Land Consolidation Bill. Although the Parliament was still young, and there was no reason to believe that it did not fairly represent the views of the country upon the question at issue, Sir Henry obtained a dissolution from Lord Augustus Loftus, who is credited with having had no opinion independent of his Premier since his arrival at Government House.

The General Elections have resulted in an enormous majority for the Opposition, and Sir Henry has resigned with the worst possible grace, having forfeited any regret that might have been felt for his overthrow by the abuse which he lavished on his opponents when he saw that the elections were going against him, and the ridiculous pomposity with which he has told the electors that they were not educated up to appreciating him. As to the cause of his fall, it may partly be attributed to the opposition of the Roman Catholics or denominational-education party, and of the publicans; but it is chiefly due to a strong feeling throughout the colony, that the land policy inaugurated by Sir John Robertson, just twenty-one years ago, has proved a failure, and that it has raised up a warfare between the pastoral tenants and the agriculturists, without any adequate advantage to the latter.

It is passing strange that the colony, which was the first to introduce the democratic land system of 'free selection before survey' into Australia, should be the first to abandon it; and that the same Minister, Sir John Robertson, who came into note through its introduction, should practically end his political career with its downfall. The faults of selection before survey were obvious from the first. The 'selector,' being allowed to purchase in any part of the colony, used often to pick out the heart of the squatter's leasehold run. It became, of course, the squatter's interest to starve him out, and the selections, being isolated instead of contiguous, were ill able to battle against this opposition.

The Bill on which the Coalition Ministry was defeated was merely a digest of preceding Acts on the subject; and what contributed no little to the fate of the Ministry, both in the House and in the country, was the circumstance that not one of them, except Sir John Robertson, took any interest in the Land Reform question, and that, until his recent coalition with Sir John, Sir Henry Parkes had been one of the most bitter opponents of the measures, on the consolidation of which he staked the life of his Government. Sir John had undoubtedly taken a back seat in the Coalition Government, and it was partly to revive his failing prestige that Sir Henry Parkes brought in a measure which was notoriously indifferent to himself. His brilliant reception in Europe and on his return to Australia had turned his head, and he believed he could make the House and country swallow whatever he chose. But his vaulting ambition o'erleaped itself, and in his chagrin and mortification he has unveiled the mask of respectability which he has worn for the last few years, and given vent to language and sentiments which have seriously injured the position he was achieving and the prospects of a return to office. These should have been excellent, since the new Ministry is weak in *personnel*, and has before it the duty of framing a new land policy, which is much more difficult than that of picking holes in the existing system. For the present they have shelved the question by appointing a Royal Commission to inquire into the working of the land laws. The programme for the session, revealed in the Speech from the Throne, contains nothing more startling than amendments of the Licensing Act and Criminal Laws, and measures for the establishment of secondary schools throughout the colony, and to abate the rabbit pest.

The leading measures introduced by the Coalition Ministry during their four years' tenure of office were, if we except a Licensed Victuallers' Amendment Act, an Educational Act on the basis of that existing in the other colonies, which served as a trump-card at the 1881 general elections, and a measure for constitutional reform, in which they were checked by the Upper House in 1879. Sir Henry's object, like Mr. Berry's, was to strengthen the hands of the Assembly, but unfortunately for his scheme he had a very different class of electors at his back. As happened over the Land Act, his weathercock failed to point in the right direction. When the Council rejected his Bill, he indulged in threats and fulminations which would have done credit to a Berryite of the Berryites. But the country utterly refused to back him up. It would not be roused into indignation on one side or the other, and was utterly indifferent as to whether the Council was reformed or continued as of old.. So after a few days fuming and fretting, Sir Henry thought it wiser to let the matter drop. The Legislative Council still remains nominated by the Crown, the tenure of office being for life. On the Education Act, Sir Henry's platform was the consolidation of a system of secular education and the withdrawal of all grants in aid of denominational schools. Here, as on the Land Act, he had held other views in other times; but in this instance he caught the direction of the wind correctly and sailed before it triumphantly.

In the new Ministry there is plenty of promise but little of past performance, and withal a good many discordant elements. The Premier, Mr. Stuart, is a good business man, of education and manners, but that is all that can possibly be said for him. The Minister for Education, Mr. Reid, is decidedly able, but very young. The Attorney-General, Mr. Dalley, is a man of great literary ability and a leader of the bar, but he has wretched health. The rest of the Ministry are nonentities, and by omitting one or two men whose respectability is hardly equal to their ability, Mr. Stuart has raised himself up an Opposition out of his old following. These will probably combine with Sir Henry Parkes, and *qui vivra verra*.

The colony, of South Australia has, to my thinking, been peculiarly favoured. Conceived by political economy and born of religious nonconformity, it has ever been the most sober and respectable province of Australia. Thanks to Mr. Gibbon Wakefield's principles, on which the colony was founded, but little of the land fund has been squandered to fill the coffers of influential squatters, and by a system of credit to small freeholders in districts proclaimed suitable for agriculture--i.e., free selection *after* and not before survey-a large class of yeomanry have been established on their own farms. The stamp of the lower middle class (chiefly Dissenters) who formed the bulk of the early settlers has not yet been erased from social and political life. Never making giant strides, nor stumbling into pits of gold, like her nearest neighbour, South Australia has yet progressed year by year at an even jog-trot along the road of material prosperity. Although copper-mining has contributed no insignificant quota to the national wealth, the foundations have been laid in pasture, and the main structure is built up in wheat-growing. Owing to a combination of these circumstances, the division of wealth approaches much nearer to equality than in any of the other provinces. There are fewer rich and fewer poor. The standard of wealth is lower. The condition of the working-class is better and healthier; their chances of becoming proprietors and employers are greater. The middle class preponderates, but its very size, the diversity of interests it represents, and the stake it has in the general welfare of the country, prevent it from abusing its political power to any serious extent. Except with its aid, neither the squatters nor the working-class can gain undue advantages; and as this aid has rarely been lent without good reason there is an almost total absence of class antagonism and an excellent public spirit throughout the community, all classes working well together for the common weal.

Definite political parties there are none, except on the few occasions when a stirring question has temporarily divided the community. The spirit of the colony is thoroughly liberal, without being democratic in the narrow sense. In most important reforms--such as the withdrawal of State aid to religion; the registration of landed property; the acquiring of Constitutional

Government, and the placing of the Constitution on a liberal basis; the introduction of the credit system for the purchase of small farms, and refusal to sell large tracts of country; and the adoption of State Education--South Australia has either led the way or been amongst the first. Thanks to the more advanced views of the earliest settlers, the abuses to be done away with have never been so flagrant as in the other provinces. Hence the work of reform has in every case been carried out in a more just and moderate spirit. The chief fault to be found in the political temper of the people lies in their apathy. When they do go to the poll, not a few of the electors prefer to vote for the candidate whom they believe to have the most honesty and public spirit, even if they do not happen to agree altogether with his political views. But the preference of men to measures is by no means an unmixed evil under the circumstances. A new country not only offers great facilities for political adventure, but rarely sins by going too slow, and when any policy of real import comes to the front, the evil corrects itself in proportion to the importance of the occasion. To this preference, also, it is due that, although South Australian politics are for the most part personal, yet the evils of personality are less prominent than in the sister colonies. Political consistency is rated higher, and the tone of the debates is infinitely better, than in New South Wales, where there is the same absence of important questions. Indeed, the Legislature is famed throughout Australia as being the most hard-working and best behaved.

With regard to Free Trade, a compromise has been adopted, and there are not wanting signs of a disposition to follow the example of New South Wales; but I fear this is rather out of dislike to Victoria than from any abstract recognition of the advantages of a Free Trade policy.

Warned by the troubles to which the question of Upper House reform gave rise in Victoria, the South Australians tackled it last session, when both Chambers were on the best of terms with each other, and an Act was passed by which the franchise was reduced from £50 freeholders and £20 leaseholders, to £20 leaseholders and £10 freeholders; the tenure of a seat shortened from twelve to nine years; the colony divided into electoral districts instead of voting in block; and a scheme introduced for finally dissolving the Council in the event of the occurrence of certain circumstances tending to produce a deadlock. All parties were agreed as to the general principles of the Act, and beyond a little skirmishing over matters of detail, it passed through both Houses with as little excitement as any petty measure. Public opinion has also declared itself in favour of imposing a tax either on income or on property, which is felt not to be paying its fair share towards the Government of the country. A land-tax was talked of, but in view of the re-action on the land question, which has extended in a modified shape from New South Wales, and of the present distress of the landed interest, such a tax is not likely to be imposed. Certain it is that additional revenue to meet the interest on the money borrowed for public works must be raised from some source. The land revenue, which had been used for ordinary revenue purposes, is now beginning to drop; and since the colony is but slightly taxed, in comparison with its neighbours, it has no reason to grumble at an increase of taxation. Amongst the more important measures passed last session, was one for providing compensation for improvements to selectors surrendering their agreements, and for remission of interest to those who have reaped under a specified average during the last three seasons. Another sets apart a million of money for making a railway to the Victorian border to place Adelaide in communication with Melbourne. The distressed condition of the selectors, who have taken up land in country which all experts pronounced unfit for agricultural purposes, except in exceptional seasons, will necessitate a measure next session to give special advantages for improved cultivation. Here also, as in New South Wales, the antagonism between the squatter and the selector, though less pronounced, is beginning to be found artificial. Owing to the clause in nearly all pastoral leases which provides for the resumption of all lands leased for pastoral purposes at three years' notice, and the want of inducements to capitalists to open up the interior, local capital is travelling over to Queensland. The probability is that the impossibility of selection beyond a certain area will be recognised, and special inducements will be offered to persons wishing to depasture unused land in the centre of the continent. There is some talk of a trans-continental railway between Adelaide and Port Darwin, which a syndicate has offered to construct on the land-grant system. But it looks as if the Government, which will never for years be able to construct the line itself, were unwilling to allow anybody else to do it.

The present Ministry, like its predecessor, which lasted four years, is eminently respectable. The Premier, Mr. Bray, has shown himself to be one of the best leaders of the House ever known in Adelaide. The Minister of Education, Mr. Parsons, is distinctly able. The Treasurer, Mr. Glyde, represents caution, and the Minister of Public works, Mr. Ramsay, shrewdness and enterprise. Altogether it is a strong combination of administrative ability, and in Messrs. Bray and Parsons it has two good speakers. It cannot be said that the Ministry has any particular policy, though it represents the farmers and working-classes rather than the propertied section of the community. It will probably make use of the recess to find out what proposals are likely to meet with least opposition, and the Opposition will pronounce no definite opinions till the Ministry have made up their minds. And this is the chronic state of affairs. On minor differences Governments go in and out, but the broad lines of policy are laid down by the country, and remain the same whoever may be at the head of affairs.

Nowhere is the theory of government by the people more fully and fairly illustrated.

To write with any comprehension on the politics of a country, one should have lived in it and be acquainted with the principal actors on its political stage. A mere visitor's impressions must necessarily be superficial, however much they may be backed up by reading. Hence, I shall only say as much about Queensland as is absolutely necessary to the rest of my subject. Originally Moreton Bay was a branch penal settlement of New South Wales, and as only the worst and most troublesome characters were sent there, the history of the district up to the cessation of convict immigration in 1839, was none of the brightest. The discovery of the Darling Downs led to a certain amount of pastoral settlement, but it was not till its separation from New South Wales, in 1859, that, Queensland really began to flourish. Ever since, with the exception of two short periods of depression in 1866 and 1877-78, the youngest of the Australian provinces has been catching up its elder sisters with rapidity. The northern half of the colony offers unlimited opportunities for growing sugar, cotton and other semi-tropical products; and the area is so vast that there are not wanting prophets who say that Queensland will, twenty years hence, be the leading colony of the group. It is more than probable that, long before that period, she will have split up into two provinces--the older and southern settlement resembling New South Wales in character, and the more recently occupied northern district, with its semi-tropical industries, forming a half-way house between Australia and India. A country of squatters and planters is naturally Conservative in its politics. This is the only colony where manhood suffrage does not obtain, the qualification for the franchise being £100 freehold or £1 leasehold. The members of the Upper House are nominated by the Crown for life.

The political parties of the day may be said to represent the interest of Northern and Southern Queensland respectively. The Ministry, at the head of which is Sir Thomas McIlwraith, represents the Northern portion. Hence they have recently signed a contract with an English syndicate for the construction, on the land-grant system, of a trans-continental railway to join Townsville and other north-east coast settlements with the Gulf of Carpentaria. Reproductive works and free immigration form a principal item in their policy; but that which has attracted much opposition is a proposal for the introduction of regular supplies of Cingalese. The Opposition, led by Mr. Griffiths, represents the cooler climes, where coolie labour is little wanted, and which cannot be benefited by the railway. These contend that it would be impossible to confine the coolies to the sugar plantations, and that they will interfere with the legitimate labour of Europeans. They look for the support of the working-classes. The Northern interests are those of planters and capitalists.

Although Western Australia occupies a third of the total area of the continent, it has so little connection with the sister colonies that it can hardly claim to be considered as a factor in Australian politics. The colony was founded in 1829, under the name of the Swan River Settlement, by a number of gentlemen, many of them retired officers, to whom the Imperial Government gave far larger land grants than they had capital to manage. For twenty years both settlement and settlers had to struggle for bare existence, until in 1851 they persuaded the Home authorities to establish a convict station there. This supplied much-needed labour for public works and a market for the stock and produce of the settlers, while the maintenance of the convicts necessitated the expenditure of £80,000 to £90,000 a year of Imperial money in the colony. With these aids, the settlers kept their heads above water, till, owing to the Victorian outcry against what was termed 'a blot' on the already rather shady 'escutcheon' of Australia, the immigration was stopped in 1868. Since then the convicts have dwindled down from 5,000 to 500. Happily the discovery of new pastoral lands occurred almost simultaneously with the cessation of convict immigration, and the colony has slowly but gradually progressed, until now it has a population of 30,000 inhabitants. During the past year exploration has been vigorously prosecuted. Large tracts of country have been taken up for pastoral purposes by capitalists in the other colonies, and several projects for the construction of railways, to be paid for by grants of land, are now under consideration by the Government. At the present moment nothing but capital and population of a more energetic kind than the old settlers seems to be wanting for Western Australia to become a prosperous colony; and provided he is not afraid to rough it, there is no part of Australia in which a capitalist--whether large or small--can more remuneratively settle than in this out of the way part of the world; and this I say after having myself temporarily lost heavily there. Capital is the great need of Western Australia. At present, you feel yourself more out of the world in Perth than in Siberia. The people are poor, old-fashioned, warm-hearted, and slow-going, with no belief in the resources of their own country. Whatever wealth is made there, is made by outsiders-- mostly Victorians--who are gradually galvanizing the place into life. But that Western Australia is destined to become a great country, no one who has lived there long enough to know something of it, and not long enough to become impregnated with the prevailing indifferentism, can doubt.

The province is still under Crown Government, although there is a Legislative Council, two-thirds of the members of which are elected by £10 householders, which is yearly gaining power. The advent of Constitutional Government will depend entirely upon the progress of the colony; but at present it is far from being desirable, the elected members of the Council being distinctly the obstructive party, while the Governor and the Imperially appointed officials are the only persons who look beyond the squatting interest to that of the colony as a whole.

The politics of the country consist of discussions as to whether settlers should be bound to pay half the value of the fences a neighbour has erected or wishes to erect between them; whether the railway should be allowed to go through a certain square in the township of Guildford; whether police protection, at the expense of the whole colony, should be afforded to settlers in the outlying districts, who are exposed to attacks of natives. People living within hearing of St. Stephen's can hardly imagine the virulence with which these petty questions are gone into, still less that for months they have formed the only topics of conversation. Liliput must, I feel sure, have been a far noisier place than Brobdingnag, and with the kindest feeling towards the most hospitable people in the world, I cannot forbear a smile at the recollections of the boredom I underwent on the subject of the Fencing Bill.

Reviewing Australian politics as a whole, one notices that whilst all the colonies are distinctly 'Liberal' in their ideas, the shades of colour vary from Whiggism in New South Wales and Queensland, to extreme Radicalism in Victoria, with South Australia as the exponent of the more sober Radicals. The two more important provinces have diverged considerably from each other, partly from sheer opposition, but chiefly from diversity of circumstances and constituents. Until recently, South Australia was content quietly to beat out its own little track; but the *rapprochement* between all the colonies, which increased facilities of communication have brought about, is yearly tending to lessen its individuality and to make it a mere copy of one or the other of its big neighbours.

In discussing constitutional questions it is well to remember that, although all the Australian constitutions are founded on analogy with the British, that analogy can easily be carried too far. To begin, the main functions of the Colonial Legislature, and the relations of the two Chambers towards each other, are for the most part written down in black and white, their constitutions allowing no room for the 'broadening down from precedent to precedent,' which has enabled the British constitution to work comparatively so smoothly. The latter grew up naturally, the former were made to order. All parties in Australia are agreed to follow British precedent where none is provided in the Constitution Act; but there is a considerable party who actually hold that the colonial constitutions being modelled on the British, the spirit of the British constitution should be followed, even when it does not altogether agree with the letter of their own; and this, although it is obvious that an Upper House on such a broad electoral basis as that of Victoria or South Australia, affords almost as many points of comparison with the House of Commons as with the Lords. A peculiar instance of this feeling was shown in 1861 in New South Wales, where, the Upper Chamber being nominated by the Government, Sir John Robertson took advantage of the precedent established by Earl Grey's threat, to swamp the Legislative Council with nominees in order to pass a Land Act. Another difference besides the mode of appointment lies in the different education and social status of the members, about which I shall have something to say further on.

Happily there has so far rarely been any strain in the relations with the mother country. It may be true that the colonists are gradually getting less patient when the Queen's assent is refused to an Act, but the Colonial Office is also becoming more wary in refusing such assent. This leads on to the general question of the probabilities of a separation. Certainly there is no sign of any intention deliberately to cut the painter; but by a rash act on the part of the mother country, or if Australia were to suffer severely in a war in which she had no concern, it might suddenly and unexpectedly snap. Such I believe to be the true state of the case, unalterable either by Imperialistic demonstrations at home, or ultra-Royalistic effusions out here; although in the ordinary run of affairs neither of these are without their use in keeping up a cordial feeling. Even in semi-communistic Victoria there is at present an unlimited fund of British patriotism, and, superficially, the colonists are more loyal than Englishmen living in the land. But present it has to be remembered that a majority of the inhabitants are still English born and bred, and that the circumstances of colonial life do not encourage the indulgence of sentiment at the expense of material advantages. Where the treasure is, there will the heart be also. When the purely Australian element gets the upper hand, the keeping of the British connection will become merely a question of advantage and opportunity. In time of peace the advantage is decidedly on the side of the present state of things. The events of war might reverse the position.

No unimportant tie is the disunion between the colonies themselves. So far all attempts at Federation, whether proceeding from England or from public feeling in Australia itself, have completely failed. The subject was actually discussed at a recent Intercolonial Conference, and again last session in the Victorian House of Assembly. But I very much doubt whether all the talk that is going on upon the subject will overcome the practical difficulties within the present generation, unless there come some period of common danger. Certain it is that if Federation is to be brought about, the movement must be endogenous. At present the way is blocked by the opposite commercial policies of Victoria and Now South Wales. That practical experience will point out the true solution of the Free Trade and Protection controversy in Australia is hardly likely, when one notices the present Protectionist movements in England; but in the course of years, one may reasonably expect that a purely Australian feeling will overcome this stumbling-block, and give us one tariff for the whole of Australia. Such a feeling can hardly become sufficiently strong to effect this object without encroaching considerably on the ground now occupied by Imperial patriotism. How true this is, is exemplified by the fact that the first, and so far the only subject upon which there has been any Australian, as opposed to provincial feeling, is Australian cricket, or more properly the Australian Eleven. And in connection with this I note that the matches against England are invariably called International, which is not strictly correct. The two questions of Federation and Separation are almost inseparably bound together, though in time of war a federation would be possible which would only bind Australia more closely to England. Then will be the opportunity, not only for Federation, but for Consolidation, or for Separation. Which it will be, must depend largely on the course events take. As I pointed out above, if Australia were to suffer severely, it might cause Separation; but if, on the other hand, she felt that her liberties and well-being were preserved by direct force of British arms, it is quite probable that an irresistible feeling in favour of Consolidation might arise, and Lord Carnarvon's dreams might be realized, provided the British Government struck the iron while it was hot.

When Federation takes place, I think there can be little doubt that it will take a shape similar to that of the United States; and that in due course of years Federation, in this shape, will become a fact, seems to me more than likely. Sir Henry Parkes's idea of fusion seems applicable enough to Victoria and New South Wales, if they could overcome their economical enmities; but that South Australia or any part of Queensland should join is impracticable. A year in New Zealand has been sufficient to convince me that the abolition of the Provincial system there has been far from an unmixed benefit. For most purposes, the colony of New Zealand is merely a geographical expression. If the distances between Dunedin, Christchurch, Auckland, and Wellington are sufficient to mar the fusion of the New Zealand Provinces, how infinitely more impracticable would a central Government at Albury be so far as Adelaide and Brisbane are concerned.

The character and behaviour of the members of Australian legislatures have to be considered in forming any just estimate of colonial politics. Unfortunately, the little that is known on the subject at home has revealed neither in a favourable light. The rowdy members and rowdy scenes have *ipso facto* attained prominence; but after carefully watching for myself, and taking the opinions of those best qualified to form them, I cannot but think that the generally-received opinion even in Australia is incorrect, and that, taking all the circumstances into consideration, both character and behaviour are far better than one has reason to expect. Here, as in many other respects, Victoria is the most pronounced example of what may be called Australianism as opposed to Englishism. Up to the present moment, she is the only Australian colony (I do not count New Zealand) which pays her legislators, and consequently she has at once the cleverest and the worst-behaved set. There are very few members of her parliament who can claim to possess any real political talent. But the general average of native as apart from trained ability, and of clearness in expressing what they wish to say, will--if we except the dozen leading men on each side of the House of Commons--compare with that of the more august assemblage. Nine-tenths of the Victorian members possess at least the gift of the gab. In the excitement of the moment, grammar goes to the winds, and h's fall thick as leaves in Vallombrosa, but they neither hesitate nor falter in their speech, and are nearly all possessed of a good deal of useful practical information. Their behaviour is certainly open to exception, but so is that of the House of Commons. The only difference is, that in Melbourne bad behaviour is almost the rule, while at St. Stephen's it may be considered the exception. Ministers and leaders of the Opposition give each other the lie direct and think nothing of it, and unparliamentary epithets are freely bandied about. At times there have been scenes unsurpassed only in the French Assembly, and one or two members have kept up a continued fire of uncomplimentary interjections. But it is only fair to remember that the great majority of the House belong to the lower middle class, and are found wanting, even if judged by the not very elevated social and educational standard of the colonies. Many of them have risen to their present not very high estate from the lowest class. Amongst people of that kind you cannot expect to find the tone of the House of Commons. The unfortunate members cannot leave the manners and customs of their class in the cloakroom of the House. Besides this, the questions under discussion in Melbourne of late years have been particularly inflammatory. When the appeal has been made from reason to passions on the one side, and to pockets on the other, the debates can hardly be anything but stormy; and if one recollects that most of these encounters take place between the present and the past lower orders, is it astonishing if irony and sarcasm give place to Billingsgate?

The recent exposure of grave political scandals in Sydney has attracted attention to the seamy side of the political life of the colonies. But such scandals, I would fain believe, are exceptional. The tone of the Sydney House is little, if at all, better than that of the Melbourne one, in spite of the members being unpaid. Political adventurers--the curse of communities like these--are perhaps not so numerous, for the £300 a year paid to every Victorian M.P. offers special facilities for the professional politician, but some light has recently been thrown on their misdeeds. The questions under discussion in Sydney are also less important. But the very unimportance of New South Wales politics leaves open a wide door for strong language. I have a vivid recollection of hearing one member talk about the 'effluvium which rises from that dung heap opposite,' alluding to another member, who fortunately was well able to return the compliment in kind. Both, however, are amongst the most useful men in the House. Such amenities are mere matters of everyday occurrence, ripples without which the debates would stagnate. The pity of them is that they discourage men of education and position from descending into the political arena, and even corrupt the manners of those who do. Still, one must bear in mind that, however much a low tone is in itself regrettable, it is no criterion of the work of which the House is capable and which it actually gets through.

In South Australia the tone of the House is much higher than in any of the other colonies. The general standard of ability is not so high as in Victoria, but the social status and general respectability of the members are considerably higher. The House seems to be impressed with the idea that it is considered the most respectable in Australia, and to strive to maintain its reputation in that respect. So mild is the general tenour of the debates, that an old House of Commons reporter assures me that the South Australian Assembly is a more orderly body and far more obedient to the Chair than St. Stephen's. Personalities of the warmer kind are considered bad form, and one of the ablest men in the House has completely lost all political influence from the shadiness of sundry transactions which, in the sister colonies, would most assuredly have been forgiven long before they were forgotten. Of course the House is hot free from adventurers, but they are of the better type, and have to conform to a fairly high standard of political morality, if they wish to obtain office and influence. As I stated before, the absence of burning political questions, and the peculiar temperament of the colonists, has led to a reputation for respectability being the chief recommendation for a seat in the House. There is occasionally a little 'log-rolling' to obtain the construction of public works in particular districts, but like everything else in South Australian politics, this is very 'mild,' and the struggle between the districts is never sufficiently strong to interfere seriously with the common weal.

In Queensland, in spite of a Conservative constitution, the debates, if we may believe the fortnightly letters published in the leading papers of Sydney and Melbourne, rival those of Victoria in rowdyism. Personal animosity between members runs to an unpardonable height, and the leaders of the two parties are constantly making accusations against each other's integrity. Political scandals are more numerous, if less important, than in Sydney. Altogether, the impression that I have gathered is unfavourable to the Brisbane Legislature.

The most prominent politicians in Australia are Sir Henry Parkes and Mr. Berry. Of these, Sir Henry Parkes is unquestionably the abler. He is a fair administrator, a good debater and leader of the House, has statesmanlike ideas, and but for his overweening conceit might have risen to the rank of a statesman. Mr. Berry's talent lies in a fluency of specious but forcible speech appealing to the mob, rather than in debating power. His vision is limited, and he is a poor administrator. After these two I would place Mr. J. G. Francis, now the leader of the Victorian Conservatives, who is decidedly able, and Sir John O'Shannassy, whose adherence to the Catholic claims alone keeps him out of a commanding position. Sir John Robertson may perhaps claim to be placed before either of these two, but it must be upon the ground of past performances rather than of present action; he is emphatically a light of other days. Sir Bryan O'Loghlen will never do anything remarkable; and the same may be said of Mr. Stuart. South Australia has two good administrators in Messrs. Morgan and Bray. The latter has developed during his Premiership abilities for which no one had given him credit. As a leader of the House, he has raised tact to the dignity of a fine art. Mr. Patterson seems to me the ablest of the Victorian Radicals. Mr. Parsons, of Adelaide, should also make his mark. In Mr. Ward, South Australia possesses the most brilliant speaker in the colonies but he has not sufficient application or steadiness to become powerful. Mr. D. Buchanan, of Sydney, is also clever, but his tongue runs away with his discretion. Sir T. McIlwraith, Sir T. Palmer, and Mr. Griffith, in Queensland, should of course be included in any list of prominent politicians of the day, but unfortunately I do not know enough about them to pronounce any opinion upon their abilities which would be worth having. Amongst living politicians who are not now taking part in politics, but whose names deserve to be mentioned, are Mr. Service, Mr. Murray Smith, and Sir Charles Sladen, who throughout the Reform agitation were the pillars of the Conservative party in Victoria, and Mr. Douglas in Queensland.

Amongst the younger band of politicians, it is not difficult to discern three Premiers *in petto*. Mr. Reid, of Sydney, only wants more parliamentary and administrative experience, and the more thorough understanding of the proportions of affairs which a couple of years' residence in England would give, to become the nearest approach to a statesman which Australia has ever seen. In South Australia, Mr. Dixon shows a great deal of promise. In Melbourne, Mr. Deakin's fluency of speech impressed me considerably. Upon him will probably fall Mr. Berry's mantle. All three of these rising politicians are young and enthusiastic, but while Mr. Reid and Mr. Dixon are Australians in the widest sense, Mr. Deakin's ideas seem to be unable to reach beyond the colony in which he was born.

The Land question, the Constitutional question, the Transcontinental-Railway question, the Coastal-Trunk Railway question, the Education question, the Immigration question, will be seen to be common to all the Australian colonies.

In Victoria and South Australia the constitutional question is at rest for another decade; but though it is not at present on the *tapis*, there is every probability that within the next five years New South Wales will abandon the nominated Upper House for one elected by a propertied constituency, such as that of the South Australian and Victorian Legislative Councils. Within the same period Queensland, or at any rate the southern part of it, if it splits into two over the question, will adopt universal suffrage. Very possibly the opportunity will also be taken to make the Legislative Council elective, but probably on a much less liberal basis than in the other colonies. Five years more of progress such as she has made last year, and Western Australia will become fitted for and obtain constitutional government. The liberalizing of the Australian constitutions is entirely a matter of time, but the direction is pretty well indicated. The length of each step depends mainly upon whether it is made with the goodwill of both Houses at a time when there is no urgent demand for reform; or whether it is affected by obstruction on the part of the Upper House; or whether, as seems likely to be the case in New Zealand, it is brought about by the apathy of the Second Chamber. I doubt, however, whether even Victoria has reached finality in its Constitution, and it is difficult to prophesy what form the Colonial Legislative Council of the future is to take. Probably before Reform can take a new direction, there will be Federation, with an Australian Senate.

Many people think that the solution of the Education question remains to be found. A Royal Commission was appointed last session in South Australia to consider the bearings of the existing system, and in Victoria there is already a strong political party opposed to it. After such a complete reversal of a policy which was supposed to be so firmly established as Sir John Robertson's land system, no system in Australia can be said to be finally established if there is any considerable number of sufferers by it. Most sensible people--though they are certainly not numerous--admit that the Catholics are really aggrieved by being obliged to contribute towards a system of education of which they cannot avail themselves, and many others regret the omission from our educational system of so important an element as religion. But the advantage of an uniform system of State education is widely and generally appreciated. The present system may be modified so as to give ministers of religion greater opportunities for doctrinal teaching out of hours, and to allow of broad Christian morality being taught as part of the educational course. But I cannot think that a return to State aid to denominational schools is at all probable; and if the next half-dozen years pass over without such a change, the number of electors educated under the existing system will make it impossible. The Church of England was the only Protestant body which originally objected to the secular system, because none of the other Protestant denominations had schools of their own. Now these are beginning to awake to the fact that the secular schools are thinning their flocks, and producing a large number of freethinkers in fact, if not in profession. They are therefore openly becoming more inclined to joint action with the Anglicans, not for the establishment of denominational schools, but for the introduction of broad Christian teaching into the existing schools. The Catholics, of course, hold that just as the existing schools negatively produce Free-thinkers by the absence of any Christian teaching, so broad Christianity would be mere Protestantism; i.e., the negation of Roman Catholic doctrine.

On the Land question we seem as far as ever from finality. The reaction against the selection system will probably not extend to Victoria because the quantity of land there is limited, and its character for the most part superior. In South Australia the solution will probably be in superior facilities for opening up the interior or unoccupied lands, greater fixity of tenure to the leaseholders, restriction of the land open to the operation of the system of selection, easier terms to the selector, and greater encouragement to both selector and leaseholder to improve their holdings. In New South Wales the change must be more radical, because, in the absence of the South Australian clause which made survey precede selection, the evil which has arisen is much greater. But the direction of the change will probably be similar, though the selector will be less considered, and there is not much totally unused land needing pastoral occupation. In Victoria the selections are now being increased in size to one square mile, and I think changes will gradually be made which will make the large freeholders find it to their advantage to sell. In Victoria and New South Wales there is a quantity of freehold property used for pasture which is well fitted for agriculture. South Australia, on the contrary, has pretty well reached the margin of cultivation, and must seek to improve her wheat-yield, not so much by enlargement of the area cultivated, as by improvement in the cultivation of the area already under crop.

Victoria has completely abandoned Government immigration, but New South Wales, South Australia, and Queensland each grant free or assisted passages to immigrants of a certain class. For the last three or four years the immigration policy has been slackened, but there is every sign that another push is going o be made in this direction by South Australia, which had almost entirely stopped free passages, and by Queensland. Beyond question, one of the chief needs of Australia at the present moment is a steady stream of immigration, and this can only be obtained by more strenuous efforts on the part of the Colonial Governments to make the position and prospects of the country better known at home. Immigration raises the revenue and helps to pay off the interest on our debt. It reduces the expenditure proportionately to the population. It gives more employment, since the new-comers must be housed and clothed and live; and it supplies more labour, enabling fresh country and new industries to be opened up. Population is the chief element of wealth and progress in a young country like this.

The contract which the Queensland Government has just signed for the construction of a railway from Charleville and Point Parker marks the beginning of an era of transcontinental railways constructed by English companies upon the land-grant system. The next will probably join Albany (King George's Sound) to Perth, and the third will traverse the continent from north to south, i.e. from Port Darwin to Port Augusta, and practically to Adelaide. The advantages of the land-grant system are yet insufficiently appreciated in Australia, but in this system I believe there lies an enormous source of wealth. The Colonial Governments cannot possibly afford to construct these lines themselves; but if the contracts are made with discretion, the advantages which the companies will reap, though sufficient, will be as nothing compared with the enormous increase in the value of the remaining land, and the addition to the productive power of the colony. The railways from capital to capital will, of course, be constructed by the Governments of each colony. Sydney is already united to Melbourne, and in four years' time Adelaide will also be connected. Brisbane, Maryborough, Rockhampton, Mackay, and Townsville will all be joined in due course of time, and by the land-grant system Point Parker, on the northern coast, will be included. The next step must undoubtedly be the connection of Albany with Port Augusta on the land-grant system, and of Perth--or rather Geraldton--with the new settlements in the Kimberley district. All this, I think, we may reasonably expect to be done in the next quarter of a century. After that a line will probably be constructed across the centre of the continent from east to west, and the coastal trunk line completed along the north-west from the Kimberley district to Port Darwin, and thence to Point Parker.

Just before the last mail left with this letter, the Parkes Government in New South Wales exploded like a bomb-shell. A fortnight after it was posted, Sir Bryan O'Loghlen wrought a *coup d'état*. On the last day of January, Victoria was amazed by the altogether unexpected news that the Ministry had advised, and the Governor granted, a dissolution. The morning papers had not contained even a hint of such a catastrophe, and the publication of the Government *Gazette* containing the proclamation was the first intimation of it which anybody outside the Cabinet received. The grounds upon which the request of the Ministry was granted were, that the House was so divided into sections of parties that it was impossible to carry on the public business; that the Parliament was moribund, having only six months to live; and that the Government, which asked for the dissolution, was undefeated. Both the Conservatives and Liberals, and their leaders the *Argus* and *Age*, alike blame the Governor for granting the dissolution, on the grounds that the House was just as incompetent to transact business six months ago as now, and that the Government would never have applied for a dissolution but for the certain defeat which awaited them directly the House met, on account of the failure of the loan. To me, however, it seems that the Governor was perfectly right. Admitting the undeniable truth of the objections I have just quoted, it remains to be said that if the Government had waited to be defeated in the House, no Government capable of carrying on business could have been formed in such a House. As it is the Government are absolutely certain to be defeated in the country, and in a new House there is every chance of a strong Government being formed. Mr. Service, the ablest of Australian politicians, who led the Conservative Opposition to Mr. Berry's Government throughout the constitutional struggle, and who has been on a holiday in England during the present Minister's tenure of office, has resolved to re-enter into politics. Although a resolute opponent of the excesses of Berryism, Mr. Service is more of a Liberal than of a Conservative, and I confidently expect that the general elections will result in a Coalition Government formed of the ablest men of either side, under Mr. Service's leadership. Even Mr. Berry, in his election speech, has announced 'moderation' as his watchword, and a longing for the loaves and fishes of office will probably induce him to serve under Mr. Service. Mr. Patterson, the ablest of the Radicals, may be pronounced a certainty for the Ministry of Public Works. Mr. Francis, the leader of the Conservatives whilst Mr. Service was away, will be a fourth. For the remaining offices, Messrs. Pearson and Deakin of the Radicals, and Gillies of the Conservatives, are the most likely men. Such a Government of all the talents, with Civil Service Reform as the first plank in its platform, should rival the length and strength of the Parkes-Robertson Coalition, which lasted four years, and would be infinitely superior to it in ability. As for poor Sir Bryan O'Loghlen, the services he has rendered to the country are little likely to be appreciated at the poll, and all he will be able to do is to rally into opposition the men who think Mr. Service ought to have offered them portfolios.

BUSINESS.

The *Australian Insurance Banking Record* informs me that there are no less than 24 joint-stock banking companies, with 750 branches doing business in Australia. They all pay dividends of from 6 to 18 per cent. to their shareholders, besides putting handsome sums every year to their reserve funds, so that banking business is fairly profitable here. The existence and prosperity of so many banks in a community which, all told, is considerably smaller than the population of London, is chiefly due to the wealth of the small number of people who form it, and also to the wider range of business which the banks undertake. Nearly everybody who is worth £100 has a banking account, and most people who have an account have overdrafts, which are given for the most part on purely personal security. The banks also advance freely on growing crops, wool on the sheep's back, and all kinds of intangible security. Many of the largest merchants are to all intents and purposes mere bank-agents. It is quite a common thing for ordinary working-men to keep bank accounts; and all farmers, even the smallest, are obliged to keep them; for in the country specie payments are almost unknown, and the smallest sums are paid by cheque. Even in the towns, residents usually pay any sum over a pound by cheque. Although this practice has opened the door to a good deal of fraud, its convenience is obvious. You need never keep more than a few shillings in your pocket, and your bank keeps all your accounts for you.

In a community in which every class is largely dependent upon his goodwill, the banker occupies the highest social position, almost irrespective of his merits. It is this excessive dependence upon the banks which largely accounts for the excessive ups and downs of colonial life. In times when money is easy the banks almost force it upon their customers. When it is tight, many people who are really solvent are forced into the *Gazette*, and a panic ensues, from which it takes the country some time to recover.

The tendency to merge large firms into limited liability companies, which has extended lately from America to England, has also been felt in Australia, though not to the same extent as in New Zealand. In certain classes of business these come into competition with the smaller banks, but each, as a rule, runs hand in glove with a large bank, undertaking certain classes of loans and supplementing the bank's business. They buy wool and wheat freely in Melbourne, hold auction sales there, sell on commission in England, advance upon wool on the sheep's back and standing crops onwards; in short, merit their usual description of loan, mercantile, and agency houses. Mortgage and land investment companies are another class which has been springing up of late. One company has been started professedly to deal solely with wheat: several already exist which make wool their only concern. Besides these, there are the usual run of mining companies, which spring up epidemically and mostly have their headquarters in Victoria. It is needless to say, that in these companies it is a case of neck or nothing.

Land is naturally the safest investment of any that offer themselves in the colonies. Although every ten years or so there comes to each colony a period of intense speculation in land, with a consequent reaction, it is a generally accepted maxim, that 'you cannot go far wrong in buying land.' There is always the chance of making 50 to 100 per cent. in the year by a land purchase, and at the worst you will get 10 to 20 per cent. per annum, if you can only afford to tide over one, or at most two bad years.

On first-class mortgages the rate of interest varies from 6 1/2 to 8 per cent. for large amounts. For small amounts 8 per cent. is always obtainable by a man who keeps his eyes open. But, beyond this absolutely secure class of investments, one thousand-and-one small chances of making large profits with little risk occur to every man who has got a few hundreds; and if he fails to turn them to account he will have nothing but himself to blame.

In the early days there was of course no distinction between wholesale and retail business, and in country towns the largest firms still keep stores where you can buy sixpennyworth of anything you want. Even in the towns the distinction is not firmly established, and many of the wealthiest importers still keep shops. Nor are the trades specialized to anything like the same extent as at home; though, in wholesale trade, they are becoming more so every day. Nearly the whole of the extra-Australian trade is still with England--chiefly London--though there is a small import trade with America and China, and export to India and the Cape. The French and Germans are both making strenuous efforts to establish a market here, and the Germans especially are succeeding. A great deal of business has been done of late by agents working on commission for English manufacturers; but most of the larger importers have their buyers in England. The tendency, however, is towards buying in Australia, although it is opposed by the large wholesale importers who are injured by closer connection between manufacturers and small buyers.

If, on the one hand, there are fewer of those old-established firms in which strict traditions of honour descend from generation to generation, so, on the other hand, the smaller size of the towns gives less scope for barefaced swindlers. And thus, if the standard of commercial morality is lower here than at home, people are not taken in so easily, or to so great an extent. Everyone is expected to be more or less of a business man, and is looked upon as a blockhead and deserving to be cheated, if he does not understand and allow for the tricks of the trade. In Melbourne the heavy protectionist tariff has brought about an almost universal practice of presenting the customs with false invoices so skilfully concocted as to make detection impossible. Within my knowledge this practice has been resorted to by firms of the highest standing. Sharp practice amongst respectable firms is also very common, and verbal agreements are less trustworthy than in England. You are expected to be on your guard against being 'taken in;' and if you are taken in, no one has any compassion for you, the general opinion being that a man who trusts to anything less than the plainest black-and-white is a fool.

Liberality to *employés* and in the details of business is little known or appreciated. Exactly contrary to the prevalent idea in America, the Australian merchant is most averse to casting bread on the waters with a view to its return after many days. He distrusts courtesy and liberality as cloaks for the knave, or as the appurtenances of the fool. Loyalty is a phrase little understood, and the merchant leaves as little to his clerks' honesty or honour as he can possibly help. In business he holds that 'Every man's hand is against his neighbour, and his neighbour's against him;' and he pushes the aphorism to its fullest logical conclusion, i.e., not merely to 'Believe every man to be a knave until you find he is honest,' but 'Believe that when a man is honest it is merely the more successfully to carry out some rascality.'

The old-fashioned English prejudice against bankruptcy has been improved out of existence by the speculative nature of all business, and the consequent frequency of insolvencies. Some of the largest merchants have 'been through the Court,' as it is termed, more than once; and provided there has been no open swindle in the case, no opprobium attaches. Even when there has been swindling, it is soon forgiven and forgotten. A man who has been caught swindling is denounced at the time with an exaggerated ardour which would make a stranger think that swindles were almost as rare as the cases in which they are discovered; but it is only just to recognise that the exposed swindler has a fair chance given him of retrieving his reputation, and perhaps of setting himself up again. The fact is, that so much sharp practice goes on, that the discovered swindler is rarely a sinner above his neighbours: he has simply had the bad luck to be found out. If half the stories one hears are true, half the business people in the colonies must be more or less swindlers in small matters. I don't mean that they commit legal swindles, but merely what may be called dirty tricks. On the other hand, I know many business men in whose probity I could put full confidence. But you require to live in a place some time, and must probably buy your experience pretty dearly, before you find these out. And even they in many trades cannot help contamination. It is very difficult to mix thoroughly in business without dirtying your hands; it requires no ordinary moral courage to keep them clean when there is so much filthy lucre about. A man who is determined never to diverge from the strict path of honour finds himself of necessity at a disadvantage in the commercial maze, and the best thing he can do is never to go into it. His sense of what is right cannot but be dulled by the continual grating of petty trickery. He is led almost before he knows it into things from which he recoils with disgust, perhaps too late to prevent them, and he has continually to be on the watch for and to combat the trickery of others. I cannot say that, generally speaking, I have much sympathy with the somewhat smug self-righteousness of Young Men's Christian Associations, but I must say that they have done a great deal of good in putting a leaven of honesty into the commercial lump.

The way in which a man changes his trade and occupation is remarkable. One year he is a wine-merchant; the next he deals in soft goods; and the year after he becomes an auctioneer. The consequence of this is, that, although colonists acquire a peculiar aptitude for turning their hand to anything, and a great deal of general commercial knowledge, that knowledge is for the most part very superficial. This accounts for the phenomenal success which a newcomer who is a specialist occasionally meets with in a line of business in which he is an expert, and also for the failure which often attends the efforts of competent specialists, who become discredited because they are not able to do something properly, which in England would not be considered to come within their province. To a man coming here to establish himself in any business I would always give the advice to take a subordinate position for a year in a similar business already established. This will give him what is called 'colonial experience,' for want of which many an able man fails at the threshold.

Amongst the peculiarities of colonial trade is a strong preference for local manufactures, with the exception of wine. A large manufacturer of agricultural machinery, who has just been making a tour of the colonies, tells me that he finds merchants actually prefer an inferior and dearer article locally made, if it appears at all equal to the English one in appearance. In a certain measure I believe this to be true. It is not merely a patriotic or protective feeling of sentiment, but is to a great extent due to the untrustworthiness of European manufacturers, who constantly send out articles inferior to those ordered. The French in particular sin in this respect. The Americans seem to be most to be relied upon. Owing partly to the duty on wool, and to the small number of articles which can be exported to America, there is not nearly so much trade with the United States as might be expected. If freights were lower, or our social relations with America closer, there would certainly be many more American manufactures in use than there are now.

Generally speaking, it may be said that trade is far more speculative and profits far larger than in Europe. Capital requires and obtains at least half as much again in interest. The openings for profitable speculation are greater. In squatting, the losses are occasionally very large; but during a good season the gains are beyond all English conception, if the rate of increase of the flock, which is sometimes from 100 to 120 per cent., be taken into consideration. You hear people say that the day of the squatter is coming to an end in Australia, and that money can no longer be profitably invested in sheep-runs. If this be so, how is it that nearly every Melbourne merchant is also an owner of stations? That sheep-farming can no longer be carried on with so small a capital as in the early days may be true; but if a man has the experience, and can endure the hardships of taking up new country, he has still every prospect of success. It is in the towns only that the acquisition of wealth is becoming more difficult; but it may be laid down as a general rule, that in town or country any man with over £5,000 will, if he goes the right way to work and has ordinary luck, multiply his capital by twelve in less than a score of years; and that the impecunious man can at least find more elbow-room than at home. Clerks are said to be a drug in the market; but that is a mere *façon de parler*, expressing the fact that they are the worst-paid class in Australia. It does not prevent them from getting better pay for less work than they do in England.

In the professions, as may be imagined, first-class men are rare. When we get them, it is either on account of their health or their habits. A first-rate man can do better in England than here, not only because the field is wider, but because the standard of comparison is higher. Even a second-class man should do better at home in the long-run, though for immediate results there is no place like Australia. But the man who will do well to emigrate is he who is just above the ordinary rank and file--the *junior optimè* of his profession. The rank and file will probably do better out here, but not so much better as to compensate them for the change of scene and life; and the Australian public will take little account of a man who cannot show ability in some direction. For specialists there is not yet much scope. Our social organism has not yet become sufficiently heterogeneous, as the evolutionists would say, though it is gradually progressing every day.

Of all the professions, medicine certainly is the best remunerated. It is not merely that a certain Melbourne surgeon--a man, however, who would have made his mark in London--is making from £8,000 to £10,000 a Year, and several other leading doctors from £4,000 to £6,000; but that the general average income is about £2,000 a year, and an unknown M.R.C.S. can within a month of his landing walk into a practice of £600 for the asking. Exceptions of course there are to the prevailing high rate of income; but they proceed mostly, not from incapacity--for there is plenty of that at £2,000 a year and of drunkenness also--but from an unwillingness to begin with the hardships of a bush life. To start well from the first in town is possible, as has been proved, but only under exceptional conditions; whereas the most mediocre medico, with a mere license from Apothecaries' Hall, can land himself in a good country practice. Provided he can stand that life for three or four years without becoming a drunkard or breaking down in health, his fortune is made. At the end of that time he either takes an opportunity to buy a town practice for a small sum, which, if he has either friends or ability, is his best course, or if he has neither, he stays up in the country, and equally obtains a fortune, though with much harder work. Bush fees are large, but bush work is hard. The bush doctor may at any moment be called upon to ride fifty miles to see a patient. In town he would only get a half-guinea fee, or in Adelaide only five shillings; but the circle is circumscribed, and it is astonishing how many five shillings can be obtained in a day.

In Melbourne and Sydney the bar still exists as a distinct institution. In Adelaide, solicitors, attorneys, conveyancers, proctors, barristers, are all united, and this reform, which works admirably, will probably soon be extended to the other colonies. What generally happens is, that one man with a penchant for the forum goes into partnership with another whose forte lies in the office; and thus, though all lawyers meet on an equality, the two branches of the profession practically remain apart. But the new régime offers great advantages to juniors, who are thus no longer dependent upon attorneys, but are brought face to face with their clients. The latter, in whose interest the reform was chiefly made, have thus, also, far more freedom of choice as regards their advocates. Comparatively easy as it is for a junior to get a fair practice, the bar has too few prizes to make it worth the while of the best men to stay out in Melbourne and Sydney. There are a few exceptions, but very few, who make over £4,000 a year, and in New South Wales the Chief Justice only gets £3,000 a year. Hence a marked weakness in the colonial bench of every colony, except Victoria, where the salaries are higher. Here and there you see a first-rate judge, but for the most part judges are ex-attorney-generals of the administration which happened to be in office when the judgeships fell vacant. Political distinction has become a *sine quâ non* for a candidate for the bench. The leading counsel often would not accept the office if it were offered them, and thus the just-above-the-averages form the majority of judges.

The worst paid of all professions are the clergy, and not only are they the worst paid, but the hardest worked. The bishops get from £800 to £2,000 a year, but there are very few clergy whose stipends exceed £600, and the majority live and die without getting any higher than the £350 to £400 stage. Nor have they here the social compensation which they enjoy in England. There is no Established Church, and their position is not many degrees superior to that of the ministers of other denominations. The latter, whose wants are naturally less, are quite as well, and on the whole probably better, paid. If they have any ability, £500 to £700 is easily within their reach, and one or two distinguished preachers get as much as £1,500 to £2,000.

SHOPS.

The principal shops are noticeable for their size and the heterogeneity of their contents. At first I used to think that this want of specializing was a relic of the days of 'general stores,' which still reign supreme in the country towns. But, on the contrary, the tendency is decidedly to increase the range of retail business rather than to specialize it. For instance, it is within the last five years that furniture, china and fancy goods have become attributes of all the large drapery 'establishments, and that the ironmongers have gone seriously into the agricultural machinery, clock, china and fancy goods business. Amongst these ironmongers there are two shops--Lassetter's at Sydney, and McEwan's in Melbourne--which would attract attention in London; and in Adelaide, Messrs. Steiner and Wendt's silver-ware and jewellery shops have a style of their own which does them immense credit. But, on the whole, Melbourne is *facile princeps* in shops as in everything that may be said to enter into the ladies' department. The windows' in the fashionable part of the town are dressed anew every week, and with a taste which reminds one of Paris. But in spite of this, the best class of articles are difficult to get, and the few shops that keep them charge almost ridiculous prices. One would suppose that a better class of things would be obtainable in free-trade Sydney than in protected Melbourne, for while freights and commissions fall equally upon the just and upon the unjust, an *ad valorem* tariff such as that of Victoria presses very hard upon high-priced goods. But, as a matter of fact, the metropolitan and fashionable character of Melbourne more than counterbalances the tariff; and, so far as I can judge, you have as good if not a better chance of getting an article *de luxe* in the protectionist as in the free-trade city. Of course the latter is the cheapest, but by no means so much cheaper as the difference in tariff would imply, competition being much keener in Melbourne.

In Sydney, however, there is less adulteration and palming off of inferior for good articles. A curious instance of this came under my notice. Shortly after a recent imposition of an extra five per cent upon boots, I bought a pair exactly similar to some I had previously got at the same shop. The charge was exactly the same as before; and on my asking the shopman how it was possible for him to avoid raising his price, he candidly told me that people were accustomed to pay a certain price for a certain article, and that therefore he had been obliged to order an inferior boot, made to look exactly the same. 'My customers won't pay more, sir,' he added; 'and if I were to stick to the same quality as before, they would go to other shops, where they could get an inferior boot, looking just as good, for the old price.'

Although there are some dozen places in Melbourne and half-a-dozen in Sydney which are equal, if not superior, to any in Birmingham or Manchester, the general run of colonial shops are little better than in English towns of equal size, and their style is as English as English can be, especially the smaller shops.

But in one respect there is a great difference. The English shopman generally knows his business thoroughly, the colonial rarely. Supposing, for instance, you want some article of ironmongery in an English shop, the attendant shows you an assortment to choose from, pointing out the special merits of each variety of the article as made by different manufacturers, and guiding, but not presuming to dictate, your choice. The colonial, on the contrary, begins by asking an exact description of what you want; and then, feeling sure that he knows much more about your requirements than you do yourself, brings you very likely something that will 'do,' but is not exactly what you want. He does not enjoy the trouble of laying before you a variety of things to choose from, and except in first-class shops he does not seem to care much whether you buy or not. The result often is, that you either are strong-minded enough not to buy at all, or so weak-minded as to take *das erste beste* that is put before you. Either is unsatisfactory. So far has this custom of knowing everything proceeded, that at a leading dressmaking establishment in Melbourne when a friend of mine was ordering a dress, the fitter after the lady had chosen the stuff, and pattern, said, 'Of course you'll leave the details to me, ma'am,' the details including the length of the skirt and all the gatherings and miscellaneous ornamentations, which make all the difference between a pretty and a tasteless dress, and in which individuality has a chance of showing itself. As regards civility in the first-class establishments, there is little difference from the obsequiousness of the old country; but what difference there is, is in favour of the colony. In the second-rate shops there is often an unnecessary assertion of the shopman's equality with his customer, and a great indifference as to whether he buys or not. In the small shops where the proprietor or his family serve you themselves, the thermometer of civility registers a rise again, though sometimes after a rough fashion.

No mention of Australian shops is complete without an allusion to the fruit and vegetable shops and markets, where every kind of fruit and vegetable can be obtained at a very low price; the varying climates obtainable within a small area enabling each fruit to remain much longer in season than in England.

AMUSEMENTS.

The change to a more genial climate and clearer skies has not been altogether without effect upon the temperament of the colonists. Like the stock from which they spring their ideas of pleasure are still limited. They are still, above all, a serious people; no disposition to abate this seriousness has shown itself, even in the rising generation. On the contrary, brought up in a country where idleness is a reproach, they have the serious side of life always before them. To 'get on' is the watchword of young Australia, and getting-on means hard work. But the more ample reward attaching to labour out here leaves the colonist more leisure. And this leisure he devotes to working at play.

That 'all work and no play makes Jack a dull boy' is already an accepted maxim, is exemplified by the numerous holidays and the way in which they are spent. There must be pretty nearly a dozen public holidays in the year. Saturday is always a half-holiday. Nine till five are the accepted hours for the clerk; half-past nine till six for the shop-assistant. The eight-hour system is generally accepted in all classes of manual labour. Some shops are open on Saturday evenings; but there is a strong movement to abolish this system. The clerk is rarely called back to work after hours. In all trades and professions the hours and work of the subordinates are much less than in England. When a public holiday falls on a Monday, Saturday for most purposes becomes a whole holiday also. Christmas Day falling on Monday in 1882, business did not begin again till Wednesday. So on Friday everybody had to lay in their stock of bread and meat to last till Wednesday morning. In wholesale business, in the professions and amongst the working-classes, the whole week from Christmas Eve to the 2nd of January is practically a holiday. It is quite useless to attempt to do any business during that period. In most places it is about Twelfth Day before things get into trim again. During the first few days of the year the work is done by half the ordinary staff The colonist certainly endeavours to get as much pleasure as he can out of existence. He has a full appreciation of the value of amusement. He is not himself amusing, but he thoroughly enjoys amusing himself.

The abundance of fine and temperate weather makes outdoor life preferable to indoor during eight months of the year. Perhaps this is a reason why the colonists live in such poor houses and care so little how they are furnished. Town-life is a recent invention in Australia; and town-life as it is known at home, in the sense that numbers of people live in a town all their lives and only go into the country for an airing, is quite unknown. The majority of the population still lives, more or less, in the bush. Our ideals are country ideals and not town ideals. For all these reasons the principal amusements of the Australians are outdoor sports of one kind or another; and if the interest taken in them proportionate to the population be the criterion, this may fairly claim to be the most sporting country in the world. In Australia alone, of all countries, can any sport be called national in the sense that the whole nation, from the oldest greybeard to the youngest child, takes an interest in it.

Cricket must, I suppose, take the first place amongst Australian sports, because all ages and all classes are interested in it; and not to be interested in it amounts almost to a social crime. The quality of Australian cricket has already spoken for itself in England. Of its quantity it is difficult to give any idea. Cricket clubs are perhaps numerable, though yearly increasing; but of the game itself there is no end. There is no class too poor to play, as at home. Every little Australian that is 'born alive' is a little cricketer, a bat, or bowler, or field. Cricket is the colonial *carrière ouverte aux talents*. As Napoleon's soldiers remembered that they carried a marshal's *bâton* in their knapsacks, so the young Australians all remember that they have a chance of becoming successors of that illustrious band of heroes who have recently conquered the mother-country and looted her into the bargain, though the idea of gain certainly never enters into their heads in connection with cricket. It may be, and it is most probable, that English cricket will soon recover the laurels which the Australians carried away in 1882; but I venture to prophesy that from 1890 onwards, the cricket championship will, except through occasional bad-luck, become permanently resident in Australia. The success of the first Australian Eleven bred cricketers by the thousand. If that eleven was picked out of, say, 10,000 men and boys playing cricket, the present has been chosen from 20,000, and by 1890 the eleven will be chosen from 100,000. Certainly, very few of these can afford to devote themselves solely to cricket; but most of them will play from five to seven o'clock through six months of the year, and on holidays, half-holidays, and odd moments through nine months. Some measure of the interest which attaches to cricket can be gathered from the space devoted to it in every paper, and the fact that during the tour of the Australian Elevens the full scores of every match they played, together with details of the more important matches, were cabled from London every day, and this at 10s. 6d. a word. At the intercolonial and international cricket matches in Melbourne, as many as 23,000 persons have, on one day, paid their shilling to gain admittance into the cricket ground, and 10,000 is about an average attendance.

The other day Parliament was most suddenly and unexpectedly dissolved in Melbourne. In a place where political feeling runs so high, the greatest excitement might have been expected over such an occurrence. But 'Reuter,' who may be considered an impartial authority, merely cabled to New Zealand, 'The dissolution.'

Chiefly owing to the impossibility of bringing about an international football match, the popularity of football is more local than that of cricket; but in Melbourne I think it is more intense. Patriotism cannot, of course, be roused when no national interests are at stake, but club rivalry is decidedly stronger. Some measure of the popularity of the game may be gathered from the fact, that the member who has sat in the last three parliaments for the most important working-man's constituency, owes his seat entirely to his prowess on behalf of the local football club. In no other way has he, or does he pretend to have the slightest qualifications. Of course there are numbers of people amongst the upper and middle classes who still have a holy horror of football as a dangerous game, and the want of unanimity in rules prevents the two principal colonies from meeting on equal terms. In the older colony the Rugby Union rules are played. Victoria has invented a set of rules for herself--a kind of compound between the Rugby Union and Association. South Australia plays the Victorian game. I suppose it is a heresy for an old Marlburian to own it, but after having played all three games, Rugby, Association and Victorian--the first several hundred times, the second a few dozen times, and the third a couple of score of times--I feel bound to say that the Victorian game is by far the most scientific, the most amusing both to players and onlookers, and altogether the best; and I believe I may say that on this point my opinion is worth having. Of course, men who are accustomed to the English games, and have not played the Victorian, will hold it ridiculous that the solution of the best game of football problem should be found, as I believe it has been found, in Melbourne. But I would ask them to remember that the Victorian game was founded by rival public school men, who, finding that neither party was strong enough to form a club of its own, devised it--of course not in its present elaborate state--as a compromise between the two. In corroboration of my opinion I would point to the facts that, while Sydney is at least as good at cricket as Melbourne, there are not a dozen football clubs in Sydney (where they play Rugby Union), as against about a hundred in Melbourne; that the attendance at the best matches in Sydney is not one-third of what it is in Melbourne; that the average number of people who go to see football matches on a Saturday afternoon in Sydney is not one-tenth of that in Melbourne; and that in Sydney people will not pay to see the game, while in Melbourne the receipts from football matches are larger than they are from cricket matches. The quality of the attendance, also, in Melbourne is something remarkable; but of some 10,000 people, perhaps, who pay their sixpences to see the Melbourne and Carlton Clubs play of an afternoon, there are not a thousand who are not intensely interested in the match, and who do not watch its every turn with the same intentness which characterizes the boys at Lord's during the Eton and Harrow match. A good football match in Melbourne is one of the sights of the world. Old men and young get equally excited. The quality of the play, too, is much superior to anything the best English clubs can produce. Of course it is not easy to judge of this when the games played are different, but on such points as drop-kicking, dodging, and catching, comparison can be made with the Rugby game; and every 'footballer' (the word, if not coined, has become commonly current here) knows what I mean when I say, that there is much more 'style' about the play of at least half a dozen clubs in Victoria, than about the 'Old Etonians' or the 'Blackheath', which are the two best clubs I have seen play in England.

Of athletic meetings there are plenty, but they do not attract much interest as compared with cricket and football. Nor can rowing be called a thoroughly national pastime, though both in Sydney and Melbourne there are good rivers. The two colonies row each other annually; and in Sydney, more especially, there is a good deal of excitement over this event. But the interest felt in rowing is not much greater than in England. It is a popular sport, and that is all.

Yachting is very popular in Sydney, the harbour being almost made on purpose for it; but yachting is only a rich man's pleasure. Lawn-tennis is as much in fashion here as at home, but it is not cultivated with the same ardour. The best players in Sydney and Melbourne would not be considered as more than third-rate at home. Bicycling is gaining in favour in Melbourne and Adelaide; Sydney is rather hilly for it. There are polo and gun clubs in all three towns, but they are, of course, small and aristocratic rather than popular.

Fox-hunting there is none; but there are hunt clubs in the principal towns who run after a drag--in Melbourne after a kangaroo, and occasionally even after a deer. The country is of course monotonous, and wants very good riding. There are no sensational water-jumps even at steeplechase meetings, the colonial horse not being accustomed to water. But it wants a good horse to get over the unvarying succession of post and rail fences. People who talk about the jumps in steeplechases at home being hard should try a run over a colonial course of 4-feet-6-inch post and rails. The horses are accustomed to it, but not so always the riders. Up in the bush there is plenty of kangaroo-hunting to be got at almost any station. The squatters often pay a shilling a head for kangaroos, and very fair sport they afford when not too numerous. The wallaby is a smaller kind of kangaroo which is also hunted.

There are snipe to be shot in Australia; but wild duck is really the best kind of shooting we get, and far more easily obtainable. They are much more varied in kind than at home. Rabbits are generally too plentiful to afford much fun. I have pelted them by the score from the veranda of a station-house in South Australia. At best they are poor sport. The kangaroos and wallaby are generally too tame. Amongst other animals shootable are the native bear--a sluggish creature looking like a small bear; the bandicoot, a small animal with a pig's head and snout; the native cat; cockatoos, parrots, eagles, hawks, owls, parroquets, wild turkey, quail, native pheasants, teal, native companions, water-hens, and the black swan and the opossum. Of these the wild turkey affords the best fun. You have to stalk them in a buggy, and drive in a gradually narrowing circle round them till you get within shot. The opossum you shoot by moonlight, getting them between your gun and the moon as they jump from tree to tree. Teal are fairly numerous. Pheasants, partridges, and quail, like the deer, were imported, and have bred rapidly; but they are not sufficiently preserved.

On fishing I am no authority; but I have always understood that the fishing in Australia was very poor. Trout are being acclimatized in Victoria, but the day of the angler has yet to come.

The population of Victoria is 880,000; of Melbourne and suburbs, within a ten-mile radius, 280,000. During the Exhibition year over 100,000 people paid a shilling, or more for admission to the Flemington Race Course on the Melbourne Cup day. The usual number on that occasion is 60,000 to 80,000. I don't know any better way of asserting Australian, and especially Victorian, supremacy as *the* racing country *par excellence*, in comparison with which England, proportionately to her population and her wealth, must indeed take a back-seat. There is not an inhabited nook or corner of Australia where an annual meeting is not got up, and well attended too. This meeting is the *rendezvous* of the whole country-side, and generally ends up with a dance, and what is colonially known as a 'drunk.'

The large number of imported horses, the care taken in their selection and the prices which have been paid in England for the best sires, are sufficient proof that for strain of blood Australia is not to be beaten in the world, whilst the progeny of this imported stock has for distance beaten the best records of the English turf. Thus while Kettledrum's 2.43 is the best time--if my memory serve me right--on record for the Epsom Derby, there have been several 2.43's in Australia, and three years ago Darebin won in 2.41 1/2. And if it be objected that the imperfections of the Epsom course account for the difference, I would point to Commotion's victory in the Champion Stakes last New Year's Day--three miles in 5.26. The times here are most carefully taken, and whilst admitting that time can only furnish a rough test of merit, the times I have mentioned are sufficient to show that colonial horses can at least claim comparison with those at home. Doubtless before long we shall see an Australian colt running at Epsom; but the difficulties of age and transit must always severely handicap any Australian horse performing on the English turf.

The Victoria Racing Club of Melbourne may fairly claim to be the premier club in Australia, and in the perfection of its arrangements and of the course at Flemington, it stands a head and shoulders above any European club. Already it has an excellent stand, and yet £30,000 have just been voted for its improvement. The lawn is perfection. The hill behind the stand would appear to have been made by nature in order to allow the half-crown public to see the finish, as well as the half-guinea folk in the stand. The course is flat as a pancake, well turfed and drained. The surroundings remind one of Longchamps. On race-days trains run out from Melbourne every ten minutes; and, as you can buy your train and race ticket beforehand in the town, you need never be jostled or hurried. Everything works as if by machinery. It would really pay the South Western officials to take a lesson at the Spencer Street Station next Cup-day, to prevent the annual scramble at Waterloo every Ascot meeting.

The V.R.C. hold three race-meetings in the year at Flemington, together with a steeplechase meeting in July. The principal meeting is the autumn meeting of four days on the second of which the blue ribbon of the Australian turf-- the Melbourne Cup--is run. One hundred and twenty-eight horses entered for this race last year, and twenty-four ran. The latter number is considerably below the average. The Cup is a handicap sweepstakes of twenty sovs., the distance being two miles, and the added money only £500. Altogether the V.R.C. gave £13,000 of added money last year, the greatest amount given to a single race being £1,000 for the Champion Stakes. Next to the V.R.C., the Australian Jockey Club of Sydney ranks; but there are four other racing clubs in Melbourne, two more in Sydney, and two in Adelaide--all holding good meetings, which are well attended and well arranged. The minor meetings in Sydney and Melbourne are, however, getting to be mere gate-money and betting affairs, and do not--with one exception--attract horses from the other colonies.

Undoubtedly the chief fault of Australian racing is the prevalence of handicaps. We do not get so many short-distance races as at home, but, unless there is a prospect of a keen struggle between two special favourites, the public will not attend weight-for-age races in numbers at all adequate to defray their expenses, while a good handicap is always remunerative. The V.R.C. does its best to hold out against popular feeling by giving liberally to weight-for-age races, but without plenty of handicaps they could not find money for the weight-for-age races, far less for the luxurious arrangements of their courses.

The colonial jockeys cannot be said to be at all equal to the English, and for really good riding one must still go to the old country; but every year an improvement is visible, and before long we may reasonably expect that Australia will have its Archer, or at least its Cannon.

On all Australian courses the ring is kept well away from the enclosure. Last year the V.R.C. obliged the bookmakers to take out licenses to ply their craft at all on the course. And this brings me to the subject of betting and gambling generally. If the Australians are a racing community, so also are they a gambling community. The popularity of the Melbourne Cup is largely due to its being the great gambling event of the year. Every township in the remote bush has its guinea sweepstake over the Cup, every town hovel its half-crown one. The bookmaking fraternity muster strong on all racecourses, and apparently make an uncommonly good living out of their avocation. All kinds of laws have been made against gambling, but they have proved utterly useless. It is estimated that over a million of money changes hands annually over the Cup. Everybody backs his fancy, if only because, unless he is a strict Methodist, it would be peculiar not to do so. One of the peculiar features of this gambling mania are the numerous guinea sweepstakes got up every year by a man named Miller and his imitators. Miller last year had £120,000 entrusted to him for thousand and two thousand guinea sweeps in the Cup alone. He takes ten per cent. for management, and the rest is divided into so much for the winner, a fair sum for second and third, and the balance amongst runners and acceptances. Even those who draw a horse at all get something. Miller has many imitators, two of whom have bolted with the money entrusted to them; but deriving so liberal an income from them--something like £5,000 a year he is hardly likely to be dishonest.

Passing from racing to horses generally. The riding capacities of the Australians are well known. Nearly every one born in the colonies learns to ride as a boy, and not to be able to ride is to write yourself down a duffer. Horseflesh is so marvelously cheap, that it is not taken so much care of as at home. In outward appearance, the Australian horse has not so much to recommend him as a rule, but his powers of endurance rival those fabled of the Arabian. A grass-fed horse has been known to go as much as 100 miles in a day.

In 1796, i.e., only eight years after the establishment of a convict settlement at Botany Bay, the Victoria Theatre, Sydney, was opened with the famous prologue--

'True patriots all, for be it understood

We left our country for our country's good:

No private views disgraced our generous zeal,

What urged our travels was our country's weal;

And none will doubt but that our emigration

Was proved most useful to the British nation.'

The author was an ex-pickpocket; the actors were all convicts, and the price of admission was the same all over the house--one shilling, payable in flour, wheat, or liquor! Such a first night must have been unique in the history of the drama.

The modern Australian stage, however, only dates back as far as 1853. How popular it had become may be judged from the fact that Melbourne has four theatres, Sydney two, and Adelaide two, besides concert halls. As in England, these theatres have nothing to recommend them outside, nor can the interior arrangements be commended. A large part of their beer revenue is derived from drinking bars which are kept in connection with them. One of these, though respectable enough, is generally unpleasantly in close proximity to the entrance to the best seats in the house, and the other forming a rendezvous for all the bad characters in the town. The auditoria are nearly all badly ventilated, and ill fitted up, the only exceptions being the Theatre Royal at Adelaide, and the Bijou in Melbourne. The approaches and exits, are for the most part poor. Boxes are unknown, and the stalls are only second-rate seats. The dress-circle, which is considered the best part of the house, consists of a kind of open gallery fitted up like the stalls of a London theatre. Above are the 'gods,' and below the pit. Prices of admission are very moderate; I have been told that during Ristori's and De Murska's visits, as much as ten shillings was charged for a dress-circle seat, but six shillings is the highest charge that has been made since 1876. In any theatre six shillings is the usual amount for the better performances, the worst only asking four, and at some theatres coming down as low as 3 shillings. Except when an Italian Opera Company is playing, full dress is unnecessary, and even unusual, at the theatre.

The colonial taste in theatrical matters follows the English pretty closely. Opera-bouffe and Gilbert and Sullivan are preferred to everything else. Next in popularity is the 'New Babylon' type of play. Low comedy also draws well; and I have often wondered that Mr. Toole has not paid us a visit. Opera pure and simple used to be more appreciated than it is; but as the companies which produced it were always very second-rate, its temporary disappearance is not altogether to be regretted. The class of opera company that usually comes out here may be imagined when I tell you that Rose Hersée was a favourite *prima donna*! There are now sufficient resident operatic singers of the third class to perform opera without assistance from European stars; but by themselves these purely colonial companies do not draw well, except in pieces of the 'Patience,' or 'Tambour-Major' type. The Byron comedies are popular throughout Australia. Thanks to a company which came out from Enaland in 1880, and most of the members of which have taken up their abode here, they have been much better acted than any other class of plays. The modern society drama is not much appreciated, partly because the life in which its action takes place is little understood, and partly on account of the lack of the class of actors required to make the pieces successful. Dion

Boucicault is still a favourite. Shakespeare is frequently played but, although the stage-mounting has been exceptionally good, and we have had such very fair actors as Creswick, and Hoskins, and Scott-Siddons, a high, authority has recently declared that Rignold's 'Henry V.' is the only Shakespearean performance, that has paid for many years.

The average quality of the acting on the Australian boards is by no means good. The difference between first and second rate art is not understood by a sufficiently large number of people to make it profitable for such companies as the Bancrofts, and Messrs. Hare and Kendall's, or stars of the first magnitude, to come out here. Since Ristori was here in 1874, Scott-Siddons, Creswick and Rignold, have been the best known actors we have seen; although Marshall's Quilp, Vernon's Bunthorne, and Hoskins's Touchstone, were impersonations of a high-class. Soldene, curious to say, did not hit the popular taste. The cardinal fault of colonial acting seems to me to be exaggeration. Most of our actors are artificial and stagey; even those who clear themselves of these faults seem to play down to the understanding of their audience. The 'star' system is as prevalent as in England. The stock companies are for the most part very poor. Pieces which require a large number of persons on the stage of course suffer. Colonial supernumeraries can only be compared with those at country theatres at home. Considering the circumstances, however, the scenery and mounting are as a rule most creditable. The last two years, especially, there has been a great improvement in this department. Melbourne is decidedly the theatrical centre of Australia. It has twice as many theatres as Sydney; most pieces are brought out there for the first time in the colonies; its audiences are more appreciative and critical; its stock companies are better. If a piece succeeds in Melbourne, its success everywhere else is assured.

Whether it is on account of the warmer climate I do not know, but certainly the colonists are a more musical people than the English. Of course I do not mean that there are any considerable number of people here who really understand classical music, or who play any instrument or sing really well. On the contrary, as I think I have said in some other connection, there is no part of the world where you hear so much bad music, professional and amateur. But it is also true, that there are few parts where you hear so much music. Almost every working-man has his girls taught to strum the piano. Amateur concerts are exceedingly popular. Most young people think they can sing, and Nature has certainly endowed the young colonials with, on the average, far better and more numerous voices than she has bestowed on English boys and girls. Sometimes when you are bored in a drawing-room by bad music and poor singing, you are inclined to think that the colonial love of music is an intolerable nuisance. Especially is this the case with me, who have been constantly interrupted in writing by my neighbour's daughters strumming the only two tunes they know--and those tunes 'Pinafore,' and 'Madame Angot.' But if you are out for a walk on a summer's evening, and look into the windows of working men's cottages, you will see the old folk after their day's labour gathered round the piano in the sitting-room to hear their daughters play. I cannot hold with those who think a working-man's daughter should not learn music. Their reasoning is illogical--for being able to play the piano is in itself harmless, and may keep the girl out of mischief. Further, it gives a great deal of pleasure to her parents and friends, and often to herself as well.

As for musical performances apart from opera, there are plenty of them. Twice a week there is an organ recital in the Melbourne Town Hall. Hardly a night passes without a concert of some kind is going on. As in theatrical matters, Melbourne takes the lead in all things musical. Last Christmas-week it was actually so ambitious as to get up a Musical Festival. The Town Hall organ is excellent. A good concert will always draw well. Ketten--who was not a marvel--had crowded houses night after night, with no other attraction but his pianoforte. Wilheling, who really deserved all the praise he got, found ample success in Melbourne, and a fair measure of it in Sydney and Adelaide. Arabella Goddard was, I believe, well satisfied with her Australian tour, though it was made when the population was not two-thirds of what it is now, and much less cultured. The colonists are genuinely fond of music, bushmen and townsmen alike. They may not know very much about it, but they are anxious to learn all they can. They will even pay to hear something above their appreciation, if the *Australasian* tells them that it will improve their musical taste. The orchestra in the Melbourne Town Hall will accommodate 500 performers, and the hall itself can seat 4,000 people. The Sydney and Adelaide Town Halls are little smaller, and yet it is no uncommon sight to see them filled whenever a good concert is provided. Besides their town halls, each city has a smaller hall, devoted to musical entertainments.

The most remunerative spectacular representation is what the most celebrated colonial impresario, Mr. R S. Smythe, calls a 'one-man show.' Mr. Archibald Forbes and Mr. R. A. Proctor both made fabulous sums out of their trip to the colonies; and if Arthur Sketchley failed, it was purely for want of a good agent. In Adelaide, which, as a Puritan community, looks somewhat askance at opera and drama, the popularity of good lectures is beyond belief.

In a horse-loving country circuses are of course popular. Perhaps in no other part of the world can a circus obtain so critical and appreciative an attendance. Christy Minstrels and conjurors apparently do well, considering how very poor some of the miscellaneous entertainments which visit Australia are, it is most remarkable that they should contrive to get so good audiences.

Household amusements are much the same as at home, although more frequently indulged in. The more frank relations between the sexes make dancing a favourite pastime. In this less pretentious social atmosphere a dance can be given without all the costly paraphernalia customary in England, and a far larger class of people are able to afford to give parties and balls. 'Assemblies' are held every season in all the towns, the season being, of course, in the winter months. Even the servants are accustomed to go to balls, and a mistress would only make herself ridiculous who looked upon their going to one as anything but proper. And here I agree with the colonists. So long as her work is done for the day, and provided that she does not go to so many balls as to interfere with her capacity for doing her work, I cannot see what impropriety there is in Biddy going to her ball. No doubt she enjoys dancing, and how can it do her any more harm than her young mistress? With all the universal love of dancing, which permeates even the strictest Puritans amongst the young colonials, there is very little good dancing to be met with. People out here do not attach much importance to what are called 'accomplishments.' To dance is pleasant, but it would be a waste of time to take trouble to learn to dance well.

A mining population is always a gambling one and a card-playing one. In Adelaide the old Puritan element still sets its face as steadily as it can against cards as the devil's playthings; but young Australia will not put up with any such prejudices. Of course the mining townships are the centre of gambling with cards; but the passion extends sufficiently widely to do a good deal of harm. 'Euchre' is the favourite game, then 'Nap' and 'Loo;' but it would not be fair to call the Australians a card-gambling people in comparison with the Californians.

NEWSPAPERS.

This is essentially the land of newspapers. The colonist is by nature an inquisitive animal, who likes to know what is going on around him. The young colonial has inherited this proclivity. Excepting the Bible, Shakespeare, and Macaulay's 'Essays,' the only literature within the bushman's reach are newspapers. The townsman deems them equally essential to his well-being. Nearly everybody can read, and nearly everybody has leisure to do so. Again, the proportion of the population who can afford to purchase and subscribe to newspapers is ten times as large as in England; hence the number of sheets issued is comparatively much greater. Every country township has its weekly or bi-weekly organ. In Victoria alone there are over 200 different sheets published. Nor is the quality inferior to the quantity. On the contrary, if there is one institution of which Australians have reason to be proud, it is their newspaper press.

Almost without exception it is thoroughly respectable and well-conducted. From the leading metropolitan journals to the smallest provincial sheets, the tone is healthy, the news trustworthy. The style is purely English, without a touch of Americanism. Reports are fairly given; telegrams are rarely invented; sensation is not sought after; criticisms, if not very deep, are at least impartial, and written according to the critic's lights. Neither directly nor indirectly does anybody even think of attempting to bribe either conductors of journals or their reporters; the whole press is before everything, honest. Although virulence in politics is frequent, scurrility is confined to a very few sheets. The enterprise displayed in obtaining telegraphic intelligence and special reports on the questions of the day, whether Australian or European, is wonderful, considering the small population. In literary ability the public have nothing to complain of.

Melbourne attracts to itself most of the able and clever men in literature and journalism There is a pleasant press club there called the 'Yorick,' which forms a sort of literary focus; and for one clever, writer whom you find in the other colonies put together, there are two in Melbourne. It is the only Australian city which can claim to have anything approaching to a literary centre. It is no wonder, then, that the *Argus* is the best daily paper published, out of England. There are people who assert that it is only second to the *Times*; but without going so far as this, there is ample room for surprise on the part of the stranger, and pride on that of the Australian, that so excellent a paper can be produced amidst so small a population, and under so great difficulties of distance from the centres of news and civilization. The *Argus* will compare favourably with the *Manchester Guardian, Leeds Mercury*, or any other of the best provincial journals. In many respects it will be found superior to them; but although the amount of reading matter it contains is often larger than in the *Standard* or *Daily News*, it cannot reasonably claim comparison with them. The leading articles are able, though often virulent; the news of the day well arranged and given in a concise, business-like manner; the telegrams--European, intercolonial, and provincial--are full, the expenditure in this department being very large. Literary articles are more numerous than in the London dailies, and are generally well executed. The theatrical critiques, though the best in Australia, are somewhat poor. The reports of parliamentary proceedings, public meetings, etc., are exceedingly full and very intelligently given, and their relative importance is well estimated. Throughout, the paper is admirably proportioned and well edited, the paragraphs being much more carefully written than in any London paper except the *Times*. There is rarely a slipshod sentence to be found in any part of the paper, which is the more remarkable as slipshod writing is a noticeable characteristic of almost every other colonial paper. The leading articles are for the most part supplied by contributors not on the permanent staff, two university professors being amongst the best known. They also write reviews and literary articles, though the doyen in that department is Mr. James Smith, to whom the *Argus* pays a retaining fee of £500 a year. Art criticism is also in Mr. Smith's hands; and although all his work is essentially bookish and wanting in originality, he thoroughly understands his subjects, and his style and language are excellent.

The paper and type used by the *Argus* are similar to those of the *Times*, and in the arrangement, contents, and general style of the paper the same model has been followed. The standard issue is an eight-page sheet about three-quarters the size of the *Daily News*; but when Parliament is sitting, a two or four-page supplement is nearly always issued; and on Saturdays the number of advertisements compels a double issue, which includes 'London Town Talk,' by Mr. James Payne, and about half a dozen columns of reviews, essays, etc. On ordinary days four to five out of the eight pages are always covered with advertisements in small type, charged for at the highest rate obtainable in the colonies. The published price is threepence, and the circulation must be from ten to fifteen thousand.

As the *Argus* may be considered as the type of the Australian press at the highest point it has yet attained, it is worth while to make a short examination of a casual copy. The reading matter begins at the left-hand corner of page 6, with the heading 'Shipping Intelligence,' under which we learn that six steamers and one sailing-ship have arrived in Hobson's Bay on December 21st, and that four steamers and one sailing-ship have cleared out. Next comes a Weather Chart of Australia and New Zealand, after the model of the one in the *Times*; and then follow the observations taken at the Melbourne Observatory, a synopsis of the weather, and the state of the tide, wind and weather at twenty-two stations on the Murray, Murrumbidgee, Ovens, and

Goulburn rivers. About halfway down the third column, we reach the heading 'Commercial Intelligence,' with a report upon the state of the market, and the sales reported during the day, auctioneers' reports, list of specie shipments, amount of revenue collected during the previous day at the Custom House (£7,498), stock sales, calls and dividends, and commercial telegrams from London, Sydney, and Adelaide.

The next heading is 'Mails Outward,' which are separated from the leading columns only by the special advertisements, of which there are over a column. It happens that this day there are only two leading articles, whereas generally there are also two small or sub-leaders. The first leader is on the finding of the Coroner's jury anent a disastrous railway accident which has recently taken place. The second on the preference of colonial girls and women for low-paid factory-work, when comparative independence, easier work, and much higher wages are obtainable in domestic service. These two leaders occupy altogether nearly three columns, and are followed by five columns of 'News of the Day,' split up into fifty paragraphs.

It is worth while to run the eye briefly through these paragraphs, which might be headed thus--*Résumé* of telegraphic intelligence; short account of Dr. Benson, whose appointment to the Primacy is announced by telegram; short account of the distribution of prizes at the Bordeaux Exhibition; announcement of the arrival of the P. and 0. mail at Albany, and of its departure from Melbourne the previous day; short account of the trip of H.M.S. *Miranda*, just arrived in the bay; ditto of the movements of H.M.S. *Nelson*, and of the Orient liner *Chimborazo*, with mention of some notable colonists arrived by the last ship; summary in eleven paragraphs of the last night's parliamentary proceedings; notice of a meeting to have a testimonial picture of Sir Charles Sladen placed in the Public Library; a puff of the coming issue of the *Australasian*; account of an inquest; three notices of Civil Service appointments; one of the intentions of the railway department about excursion tickets, and another announcing the introduction of reply post-cards; another that the Government intends circulating amongst vignerons a report and pictures of the Phylloxera vastatrix; a summary of the doings of the Tariff Commission; a notice of the intentions of the Steam Navigation Board; a list of subscriptions to the children's charities; a summary of two judgments in the Supreme Court; of a will (value £75,200); of a mining law case; of applications for probate of a will, and for the custody of children; an account of a fire, another of a distribution of prizes; a summary of the programme of a Music Festival; announcements of the different theatre performances, and seven subscription lists.

The last column of the seventh page is headed 'Special Telegrams.' Of these there are only five today: one about the construction of Prussian railways on the Russian frontier, the second about the French expedition to Tonquin, the third on the relations between France and Madagascar, the fourth noting an explosion at Fort Valerian, the fifth on the execution of Oberdank. Then follow eleven messages from Reuter on M. Tisza's speech on the relations between Russia and Austria; on the Egyptian Financial control; the new Archbishop of Canterbury; the Lough Mask murders; the health of Mr. Fawcett and M. Gambetta; the trial of MM. Bontoux and Feder; the mails; monetary intelligence; commercial intelligence, and foreign shipping intelligence. This list gives not at all a bad idea of what European news is considered of sufficient importance to be telegraphed 15,000 miles.

Turning over the page, a column and a quarter is occupied with a general summary of European news by the P. and O. mail, telegraphed from Albany. Then follows country news by telegraph. Between Sydney and Melbourne the *Argus* has a special wire, which accounts for three quarters of a column of Sydney intelligence on twenty different subjects. There is also nearly half a column from Adelaide on nine subjects, and a "stick" from Perth on three subjects. The list of overland passengers from and to Sydney is also telegraphed from Albany. 'Mining and Monetary Intelligence' takes up over a column, without counting another column in very small type of 'Mining Reports.'

Turning to the back page, we find that the first column forms the conclusion of the Parliamentary Debates. A column and a half has a large heading--'The Creswick Calamity,'--and is chiefly composed of subscription lists for the sufferers and accounts of meetings held in various parts of the country on their behalf. A column and a quarter is headed 'Sporting Intelligence '(results of small provincial race-meetings being telegraphed); a column is devoted to 'Cricket,' and a third of a column to' Rowing.'

We now take up the outside sheet, and find the whole of page 4, taken up by a report of last night's Parliamentary debates. On the opposite page (9) the first three columns contain a full report of the inquest in connection with a fatal railway accident on a suburban line. Then comes a list of eighty-seven school-buildings to be erected or completed at a cost of £25,000. Three deputations take up nearly half, and the Russell Street fire two-thirds, of a column.

Opening the sheet, pages 10 and 11 are the only two with reading matter. On 10 is a report of the Police Commission Meeting, occupying two columns and a half; and reports of School Speech Days--over three columns for eight schools. On page 11 the first four columns are Law Reports; a column and a half is devoted to a wool and station-produce report, and two half columns to reports of meetings of the Melbourne Presbytery and the Melbourne Hospital Committee.

The remaining space is taken up by paragraphs under a third of a column in length, with cross-headings as follows: 'Casualties and Offences;' 'Police Intelligence;' 'The Death of Mr. Chabot;' 'New Insolvents;' 'University of Melbourne;' 'Friendly Societies;' 'The Belfast Savings Bank Case (by telegraph);' 'The Workmen's Strike;' 'Collingwood City Council;' 'A Recent Meeting;' 'The Wellesley Divorce Case;' 'The Victoria Agricultural Society.' 'Australian Electric Light Co.;' 'Public Tenders;' 'Ballarat News;' 'Victoria Masonic Lodge;' 'Early Closing Association;' 'The Tariff Commission;' '*Iron* on Continuous Brakes;' and letters to the Editor on 'Holiday Excursion Tickets,' 'Window Blinds for Omnibuses,' 'Swimming at the State Schools,' 'The Musical Festival (3),' and 'Immigration to Victoria.'

An analysis of the advertisements of the *Argus* is almost equally interesting as showing the heterogeneity of the wants of the community. There are Births, 3; Marriages, 5; Deaths, 6; Funeral Notices, 5; Missing Friends, Messages etc., 8; Lost and Found, 13; Railways and Conveyances, 6; Shipping, no less than four columns, including eight different lines of steamers to Europe, of which six are English, and seven of intercolonial steamers, of which three are owned in Melbourne, one each in Sydney, Adelaide, New Zealand and Tasmania. The next lines are Stocks and Shares, of which there are 18 advertisements; Lectures, Sermons, Soirées, etc, 5; Tutors, Governesses, Clerks etc., 45; which may be summed up thus: Wanted, a traveller in the hardware line, cash-boys, a copper-plate engraver, canvassers, junior chemists, five drapers' salesmen, law costs clerk, an engineer and valuer for a shire council, a female competent to manage the machine-room of a clothing factory, a retoucher capable of working in mezzo crayons, junior hands for Manchester and dress departments, two first-class cutters for order trade, a good shop salesman, a junior clerk, two clerks for wine and spirit store, a clerk proficient in Customs work, two clerks, (simply), a general manager for a carrying company, a grammar-school master with a degree, and one to teach the lower classes; an organist and two medical men, £400 and £500 a year guaranteed; an accountant, private lessons in dancing, a shorthand reporter. The persons advertising for situations under this heading are only 4 out of 45; they are a matriculated governess, a dancing-master, a doctor, a singing-master.

The next lines are 'Situations Wanted,' 40; and 'Situations Vacant,' 118. The relative numbers are here again suggestive. Under the first heading I find a barmaid, three cooks, carpenters' apprentices, three gardeners, two nursery governesses, two housekeepers, three men desiring any employment, seven nurses, a tailor, and the rest miscellaneous. The vacancies are chiefly composed of 13 advertisements, from registry-offices for servants of all capacities, married couples, gardeners, housekeepers, butlers, plain cooks, parlourmaids, housemaids, laundresses, waitresses, barmaids, cooks, laundresses, general servants, nurses, needlewomen, lady-helps (3). Similar persons are advertised for by private individuals; but besides these, I find: Wanted a bullock-driver, a carter, a coachman, a shoeing smith, three butchers, a bottler, two bakers, innumerable boys, barmen, a compositor, several dressmakers in all departments, half a dozen drapers' assistants, four grooms, sixty navvies in one advertisement, millers, haymakers, woodcutters, spademen, needlewomen, quarrymen, etc., two wheelwrights, a verger at £120 a year, pick and shovel men.

Turning over to the twelfth or back page, I find Wanted to Buy, 12; Wanted to Sell, 35; Board and Lodging, 44; Houses to Let, 67; Houses for Sale, 34; Partnerships, Businesses, etc., 44, of which 12 are hotels; Wines, Spirits, etc., 16; Dress and Fashion, 3; Auction Sales, 128, taking up 12 columns; Amusements, 24, taking up 2 columns; Stock and Station Sales, 11; Horses and Carriages, 18; Produce and Provisions, 2 (Epps and Fry); Publications and Literature, 6; Bank Notices, 2; Public Notices, half a column; Business Notices, 53; Money, 41; Machinery, 23; Medical, 30; Judicial Law Notices, 6; Tenders, 26, and Meetings, 9. There is also a column and a half of special advertisements charged for at extra rates in the inside sheet just before the leading column.

Although the *Argus* has a very influential and advertisement-bringing class of readers, and penetrates beyond the limits of Victoria, by far the largest circulation in Australia is that of the *Melbourne Age*, a penny four-page sheet, published in Melbourne, which boasts of an issue of 50,000 copies daily, almost all absorbed within Australia. Its leading articles are as able and even more virulent than those of the *Argus*. Its telegraphic intelligence is good, and in dramatic and literary criticisms it is second only to the *Argus* in Australia. But its news is comparatively poor, owing to its being only a single-sheet paper, and it caters for a far inferior class than the *Argus*. Its inventive ability, in which it altogether surpasses the London *Daily Telegraph*, has brought it the nickname of 'Ananias,' and it is essentially the people's journal. Just as in politics the *Argus* is not only the organ but the leader of the ultra-Conservative party, even so the *Age* coaches the Democracy. To its influence is mainly due the ascendency which Mr. Berry's party held for so long, and the violence of the measures which poor Mr. Berry took in hand. It was the *Age* which originated the idea of the Plebiscite, and of the progressive land-tax. It is protectionist to the backbone, having commenced the cry of 'Victoria for the Victorians,' and fosters a policy of isolation from the sister colonies. Prominent amongst its leader-writers is Mr. C. H. Pearson, whose Democracy is at once the most ultra and the most cultured, the most philosophical and the most dogmatic. Another leader of the Radical party who frequently writes for the *Age* is Mr. Dakin, the rising young man of Victorian politics, who represents talent and education apart from culture.

The third morning paper in Melbourne is the *Daily Telegraph*, a penny Conservative sheet which has never attained any large influence or circulation, although edited by a man of considerable literary ability. The evening papers are the *Herald*, which is supposed to represent the Catholic party; and the *World*, which is rather American in tone, but very readable. Both are penny papers exerting very little influence.

In all the Victorian papers, of whatever party, it is noticeable that Victorian topics, and especially Victorian politics, occupy an almost exclusive share both of leading and news columns; while the New South Wales and South Australian papers devote far more attention to intercolonial and European affairs. The fact is that Victoria is much more self-contained and independent of the mother country than its neighbours. Somehow or other there is more local news obtainable, more going-on, in fact, in Melbourne than in Sydney and Adelaide put together. Everything and everybody in Victoria moves faster. Hence there is more to chronicle; and greater interest is taken in what is going on in the colony. The political excitement of the country is, after all, but an outcome of this national vivacity of disposition. Half a dozen Berrys put together could not raise one quarter of the feeling in Adelaide, far less in Sydney.

After the *Argus* I should place the *South Australian Register*, published in Adelaide, as the best daily paper in Australia. In style and get-up it is almost an exact copy of its Melbourne contemporary, and its published price is twopence. In reports and correspondence it is quite as enterprising, but its leading columns and critiques being almost all written in the office, are necessarily weaker. The whole paper is less carefully edited, but its opinions are more liberal, and it is in no sense a party paper. It May, indeed, be said that not even the *Times* exercises so much influence in its sphere as does the *Register*. It not merely reflects public opinion, but, to a great extent, leads it, and it must be admitted that, on the whole, it leads it very sensibly. It may be urged against the *Register*, that its leading articles are wanting in literary brilliancy as compared with those of the *Argus*; but they are far more moderate and judicial in political matters. The extraordinary merits of this paper, in so small a community, are due partly to its having been, at a critical period in its existence, edited, managed and partly owned by the late Mr. Howard Clark, a man of great culture and ability, and partly to the close competition of the South Australian *Advertiser*, a twopenny paper which is well sustained in every department, and noted for occasional leading articles of great brilliancy.

The *Sydney Morning Herald* is the richest newspaper property in Australia. It has correspondents in almost every capital in Europe, including St. Petersburg--where the *Argus* and *Register* are not represented--publishes an immense quantity of news, and is edited by an able and liberal-minded man.

But the absence of competition makes it inferior in enterprise to either the *Argus*, *Register*, or *Advertiser*. Its leading columns are sound but commonplace, and there is a fatal odour of respectable dulness about the paper. A second paper called the *Daily Telegraph* was established in Sydney in 1879, which seems to be meeting the wants of the penny public, but it is very inferior to the *Herald*, or to the second-rate papers in the other colonies. In Adelaide, the evening papers are merely penny reprints of half of the morning papers. In Sydney, the *Herald* proprietors publish the *Echo*, a sprightly little sheet; but the best evening paper is the *Evening News*, which caters for the popular taste and is somewhat sensational.

The wants of the bushman, who relies on one weekly paper for his sole intellectual food, and who, though often well educated, is far away from libraries or books of any kind, have given rise to a class of weekly papers which are quite *sui generis*. The model on which they are all formed is the *Australasian*, published by the *Argus* proprietors, which is still the best known and the best. Some idea of the enormous mass of reading-matter it contains may be gathered from the fact that its ordinary issue is fifty-two pages, a little larger than the *Pall Mall*, but containing five columns to the page and printed in the ordinary small type used in most daily papers, and known to printers as 'brevier.' To give an idea of the character of its contents is difficult. It is partly a newspaper, partly a magazine. The telegrams for the week are culled from the *Argus*. If it were not for the addition of a fortnightly intercolonial letter, the way in which the week's news is given would remind me of the *St. James's Budget*. It is divided into Parliament, town news, country news, intercolonial, home (i.e. English), and foreign news, and may be described as a classified reproduction of the more important news in the *Argus*.

There are generally three or four leading articles somewhat of the character--but of course not the quality--of the *Spectator*; and the notes on the first page of the Liberal weekly are evidently imitated in a page of short editorial comments called 'Topics of the Week.' 'Literature,' by which is meant a two-column review of a single book and three or four short reviews, is another heading. The 'Ladies' Column' contains a leader after the manner of the *Queen*, fashion items, notes and queries, and every other week an excellent English letter by Mrs. Cashel Hoey, dealing with new plays, books and social events in London. 'The Wanderer,' 'The Traveller,' 'The Sketcher,' 'The Tourist,' head single or short serial articles of one and a half or two columns in length, signed or not signed, but always either well written or describing something new and interesting. 'Talk on 'Change' heads a column and a half of satirical or humorous notes, which are very much appreciated, and form a more leading feature of the paper than their merit warrants. The anecdotes are often new and always admirably told, but the comments are weak. 'The Theatres' contains one general critique of the newest play in Melbourne--

sometimes two--followed by short detailed criticisms, hashed up from the *Argus*, of whatever is on the boards at the different theatres. 'The Essayist' is one of the best features in the paper, though it appeals to a very limited audience. Those written by a gentleman signing himself 'An Eclectic,' are exceptionally good--better, as a rule, than most similar essays in the *Saturday*. Dr. J. E. Taylor's 'Popular Science Notes' are by no means equal to those Mr. Proctor used to contribute. 'Original Poetry 'speaks for itself. 'Miscellany' heads a column of humorous extract paragraphs, chiefly from American papers. 'The Novelist' contains a serial. 'The Story-Teller' a single story-- original. This department is always well sustained, and no expense is spared in getting good work. 'All Sorts and Conditions of Men' has just been running through the paper, Besant and Rice being favourite authors here. James Payne, B. L. Farjeon and R. E. Francillon are other contributors whose names come into my mind. Occasionally a colonial work is chosen, and the proprietors do a great deal of service in bringing out really promising authors.

Besides all these standing dishes, there are, of course, a few stray articles on all kinds of subjects. In a copy before me is one of a series entitled, 'The Goldfields,' of special interest to miners, and treating the subject technically.

But the two departments which may be said to have made the *Australasian* are the *Sportsman* and the *Yeoman*, which, to all intents and purposes, are separate papers incorporated with the *Australasian*. Of the *Sportsman*, I don't think it is too much to say, that it is the best sporting paper in the world, not excepting the *Field*, and it fully deserves the supreme authority which it exercises over all sporting matters south of the line. The page begins with 'Answers to Correspondents.' Then come one or two leading articles on sporting matters, which form the stronghold of the department; then Turf Gossips, the Betting Market, full descriptions of all Australian and the principal New Zealand race-meetings, special training notes from Flemington, Randwick and Adelaide, intercolonial sporting notes and letters from special correspondents, winding up with 'Sporting Notes from Home.' Cricket next has a leading article and notes, followed by descriptions of the more important matches. Yachting, rowing, coursing, pigeon-shooting, hunting, shooting, football, and lawn-tennis all come in for a small share.

The *Yeoman* is not much in my line, though it is looked up to as a great authority upon all agricultural and pastoral topics. Taking a current number, I find it begins with 'Answers to Correspondents;' then comes the 'Weekly Review of the Corn Trade;' 'Rural Topics and Events;' a series of short editorial comments; a leader on' Wheat-growing;' 'The Crops and the Harvest, by our Agricultural Reporter, No. IV.;' 'In the Queensland Down County, No. VI.;' 'The Water Conservation Act, No. III.;' 'The Melbourne Wool-buyers and the Wool-brokers;' 'Separating Cream by Machinery;' 'Selling Live Cattle by Weight;' 'Fancy Price of Breeders;' 'Competition between Draught Horses;' 'Butter Cows;' 'The Black Walnut at Home.' 'Public Trial of Hornsby's Spring Binder;' 'Correspondence;' 'Horticultural Notes;' 'Gardening Operations for the Week;' 'Plant Notes;' 'Notes and Gleanings;' 'Impoundings;' etc., etc., etc.

So much for the *Australasian*, of which it must not be forgotten that the *Sportsman* and *Yeoman* are only component parts. As its name implies, it has a wide circulation beyond Victoria. In the Riverine district and a considerable part of New South Wales, it is the principal paper taken; and even in New Zealand and Western Australia all hotels and many private persons subscribe to it. To the wide area over which, and the good class of people amongst whom it circulates, is largely due the leading position which Victoria occupies in the minds of all the other colonies, and the views they take of her politics. The *Australasian* is of course Conservative, but not quite so rabidly so as the *Argus*. It surveys politics from the Conservative gallery. The *Argus* takes part in the scrimmage and leads the Conservative forces. In commenting on intercolonial politics, by which I mean those of the other colonies, it always takes a mildly Conservative view, advocating federation, caution in borrowing, and assistance to the exploration and settlement of the interior. Not its least use is, that it gives the people of one colony the opportunity of knowing what is going on in the other colonies. Many of the articles are signed with a *nom de plume*, under the cover of which atheistical and even revolutionary views are allowed to express themselves. In religious matters the *Argus* and *Australasian* maintain an eclectic attitude. Outwardly they are Christian in the widest sense of the term, but it is not difficult to see that most of their writers are agnostics. On social subjects, directly they get clear of contemporary local politics, their views are progressive and enlightened, often indeed original. It is curious to note that all the leading organs of public opinion in Australia are strongly Conservative and Imperialistic in their views of the foreign policy of England. There is only one exception, to my knowledge, the *Melbourne Age*, which advocates a non-interference policy, and would not be sorry to see 'the painter cut.' On home affairs the colonial press is naturally in sympathy with the Liberals, but the *Argus* draws the line at the Clôture and the Liberal policy in Ireland, which it opposes.

Of the imitators of the *Australasian*, the *Queenslander*, published by the proprietors of the *Brisbane Courier*; the *Leader*, published by the *Age* proprietors; and the *Town and Country*, by the proprietors of the *Sydney Evening News*, are the best, in the order named. The *Sydney Mail*, published by the *Sydney Morning Herald*, is also a good compendium of information on current topics. The *Adelaide Observer* is little better than an abstract of the S. A. *Register*, and the S. A. *Chronicle* is literally a reproduction of the S. A. *Advertiser*. But all these papers are much more provincial in tone than the *Australasian*, and have hardly any circulation outside the colony in which they are published. About two years ago a new independent paper was started in Melbourne, with the programme indicated by its name--the *Federal Australian*. It is very American in tone, and a large portion of its space is devoted to rather second-rate funniness. But the leading articles are good, and it has struck out a most useful line for itself in a supplement called the *Scientific Australian*, modelled on the *Scientific American*. This portion of the paper is of great value, and if only on that account it deserves to live.

Monthly illustrated papers are published in connection with the *Argus*, the *Age*, and the *Sydney Herald*, and also independently by printing firms in Sydney and Adelaide. The two Melbourne ones are by far the best, but they are very dear at a shilling. The same may be said of the comic papers at sixpence. The political cartoons in the *Melbourne Punch* are often excellently imagined, but the execution is not remarkable, and the reading matter is wretched. The conceptions of the cartoons are also frequently coarse. The *Society* paper has found its way here, via San Francisco. The most vulgar is the *Sydney Bulletin*, which is, as a rule, coarse to a degree; but it must be owned that it is also very clever and exceedingly readable--qualities which its imitators altogether lack. One knows quite enough about other people's business here without having papers specially to spread it, and in such small communities the *Bulletin* tribe are a public nuisance. But yet they sell freely at sixpence a copy!

The provincial press is, as a rule, feeble. Ballarat, Sandhurst, and Geelong are the only three towns large enough to support papers of the slightest value outside the place where they are published. But these small fry are very useful in their humble sphere, and are almost without exception respectably conducted. How they 'pay' is 'one of those things which no fellah can understand.'

There are a number of newspapers devoted to the promotion of the interests of the various religious bodies, the licensed victuallers, and other trades. The best of these is the *Australian Insurance and Banking Record*, which is most ably conducted. The licensed victuallers support a weekly *Gazette* in each of the principal towns. The Church of England has two organs, one in Sydney, and the other in Melbourne. The Temperance party, like their opponents, have three papers devoted to the maintenance of their views, besides which, they get a good deal of side support from the dozen or so of religious sheets. The licensed victuallers seem to combine sporting and dramatic items with the advocacy of what they call the TRADE, and abuse of the Good Templars. The latter, however, are still more vehement in abuse, and even less sensible in argument.

Besides the newspaper press, Australia possesses four magazines, two published in Sydney and two in Melbourne. Of the former, one known first as the *Australian*, and then as the *Imperial Review*, is not worth mentioning, if, indeed, it is not ere now defunct. The other, called the *Sydney University Review*, a quarterly, has only just come into existence with an exceptionally brilliant number, three articles in which are fully worthy of a place in any of the leading London monthlies. That it will continue as it has begun I should fancy to be more than doubtful. The oldest established magazine is the *Melbourne Review*, started about five years ago. For the last three years it has been languishing. The most flourishing magazine is the *Victorian Review*, which is only three years old. The contents are very variable in quality. Occasionally there is a really first-class article, and generally there are one or two very readable. The quality has much fallen off during the last eighteen months, but it affords a convenient outlet for the young colonists to air political and social crotchets, and to descant on philosophical theories. Now and then the editor used to hook a big fish, such as the Duke of Manchester, Professor Amos, and Senor Castelar, who have all contributed to its columns. The philosophical articles are naturally very feeble, but not unfrequently university professors and others among the ablest residents in Australia make the *Review* a vehicle for setting forth schemes and ideas, which would not find admission into the newspapers.

LITERATURE, LANGUAGE, AND ART.

Strictly speaking, there is not, and cannot yet be, any such thing as an Australian literature. Such writers as live in Australia are nearly all English-born or bred, and draw their inspiration from English sources. A new country offers few subjects for poetry and romance, and prophecy is by no means so inspiring as the relation of the great deeds of the past. But yet there has been at least one amongst us who may claim to have had the real poetic afflatus, and whose subjects were invariably taken from the events of the life around him. This was Thomas Gordon, the author of 'How we Beat the Favourite,' and several other short pieces of verse of rare merit, and redolent of the Australian air. George Brunton Stephens is another versifier, who at times showed signs of genius; and it is not long since a Mr. Horace Kendall died, who ran off sheets of graceful verses with considerable talent and no little poetic fancy.

In philosophy, history, and science, many of the Professors at Australian Universities have written treatises worth reading; but Australia has had so little influence either upon their subjects or their mode of treating them, that their merit cannot be claimed for this country. Perhaps the best-known writers of this class, resident in the colonies, are Professor Hearn, author of 'The Aryan Household.' and Mr. Charles A. Pearson, the historian of the Middle Ages.

Australia may boast of having furnished no uninteresting theme to Henry Kingsley, and several minor English novelists. She has sent to England no less rising a light than Mr. B. L. Farjeon; but the few novels that are written and published here have never attracted notice across the ocean, and rarely even in Australia itself, if we except Mr. Marcus Clarke's 'His Natural Life.' After Mr. Clarke come Mr. Garnet Walsh, Mr. Grosvenor Bunster, and one or two prophets in their own neighbourhood, pleasant writers of Christmas stories, clever dramatizers of novels and pantomime-writers, but none of them with the least claim to a wider audience.

The circumstances of a new colony naturally cause additions to the word-stock of the mother country. New occupations and modes of living need new words to describe them, or, as often as not, the settler not being of an inventive disposition, old words are used in a new sense.

The 'bush'--itself an old word used in a new sense--has been most prolific in new phrases. Everyone who lives in the country, whether on a station or in a farm, but not in a township, is called a 'bushman,' although properly speaking this designation only applies to a person who lives in the 'bush' or unsettled country. 'Bushranger' is another word of the same derivation, which it is needless to explain. Of course you know what a 'squatter' is. It is strange that the same word which in America is used to denote the lowest class of settlers--the man who settles upon somebody else's land and pays no rent--is here a synonym for aristocrat. The term 'farmer' is applied exclusively to the agriculturist, and a squatter would be very much offended if you called him a sheep-farmer. The squatting class in Australia correspond to the landed gentry of England. The farmer is usually legally known as a 'selector,' because under the Land Act he selects a piece of ground perhaps in the middle of the squatter's leasehold and purchases it on credit for agriculture. A 'cockatoo' is a selector who works his piece of land out in two or three years, and having done nothing to improve it, decamps to select in a new district. A 'run' is the least improved kind of land used for sheep, but the word is used almost alternatively with 'station,' which denotes an improved run. The run may be a mere sheep-walk, but a station is bound to have a house attached to it, and fenced 'paddocks' or fields. The storekeeper is the lowest official on a station. Next above him is the 'boundary-rider,' whose duty it is to ride round the boundaries of fenced runs, to see that the fence is kept in good order, and that the sheep do not get through it. A 'stockman' is naturally the man who drives the stock, and the 'stockwhip' a peculiar short-handled long whip with which he drives them. A 'cabbage-tree' is an immense sun-protecting hat, rather like the top of a cabbage-tree in shape. It is much affected by bushmen. A 'billy' is the tin pot in which the bushman boils his tea; a 'pannikin,' the tin bowl out of which he drinks it. A 'waler' is a bushman who is 'on the loaf.' He 'humps his drum,' or 'swag,' and starts on the wallaby track;' i.e., shoulders the bundle containing his worldly belongings, and goes out pleasuring. A 'shanty,' originally a low public-house, now denotes any tumble-down hut.

Apart from bush terms, there are town appellations, such as 'larrikin,' which means a 'rough.' The word is said to have originated with an Irish policeman, who spoke of some boys who had been brought before the Melbourne Police Court as 'larriking around,' instead of 'larking.' To 'have a nip' is to take a 'nobbler.' A white man born in Australia is a 'colonial,' vulgarly a 'gum-sucker;' if he was born in New South Wales, he is also a 'cornstalk.' An aboriginal is always a 'black fellow.' A native of Australia would mean a white man born in the colony. The diggings have furnished the expressive phrase 'to make your pile.' A 'nugget'--*pace* Archbishop Trench--was a Californian importation. When speaking of a goldfield a colonist says 'on.' Thus you live 'on Bendigo,' but 'in' or 'at' Sandhurst--the latter being the new name for the old goldfield town. To 'shout' drinks has no connection with the neuter verb of dictionary English. A 'shicer' is first a mining claim which turns out to be useless, and then anything that does so. There is room for a very interesting dictionary of Australianisms. But I have no time to collect such a list. The few words which I have given will serve as an indication of the bent of colonial genius in the manufacture of a new dialect; and as they are given without any effort, just as they have come to my mind in the course of one evening's thinking as I write, they may fairly be taken as being amongst the commonest.

I have headed this letter 'Literature and Art,' so that I am morally bound to say something about the latter, although there is next to nothing to say. Australia has not yet produced any artist of note. Perhaps the best is Mr. E. C. Dowling, and he is a Tasmanian. Resident in Victoria is a M. Louis Buyelot, a landscape artist of considerable merit. Excepting him, we have no artists here whose works rise beyond mere mediocrity. Mr. Summers was a Victorian, but his fame is almost unknown in his own country. Thanks to Sir Redmond Barry, Victoria possesses a very fair National Gallery attached to the Melbourne Public Library. Some of the paintings in it are excellent, notably Mr. Long's 'Esther;' the majority very mediocre. For my own part I prefer the little gallery at Sydney, which, though it has not nearly so many paintings, has also not nearly so many bad ones, and owns several that are really good, mostly purchased from the exhibitions. Adelaide has also recently bought a few pictures to form the nucleus of a gallery.

By means of Schools of Design and Art, the colonial Governments have, during the last few years, been doing all in their power to encourage the growth of artistic taste, but the whole bent of colonial life is against it. Art means thought and care, and the whole teaching of colonial life is to 'manage' with anything that can be pressed into service in the shortest time and at the smallest expense. It is only fair to mention as a tribute to the laudable desire of the people to see good works of art, that no parts of the International Exhibitions were so well attended as the Art Galleries, and that although the pictures shown there were for the most part quite third not to say fourth-rate. The press is very energetic in fostering taste, but I don't think it is natural to the people. They like pictures somewhat as the savage does, because they appeal readily to the imagination, and tell a story which can be read with very little trouble. It is significant of this, that there is hardly a hut in the bush where you will not see woodcuts from the *Illustrated and Graphic* pasted up, and that the pictures most admired at the exhibitions were those which were most dramatic--such as a horse in a stable on fire, and a showman's van broken down in the snow through the death of the donkey which drew it. Next to dramatic pictures, those in which horses, cows, or sheep appeared were most admired, for here the colonist felt himself a competent critic, and was delighted to discover any error on the part of the artist. Scenery came next in the order of appreciation, especially pieces with water in them, or verdure. Genre and figure-painting were quite out of their line.

Of Music I have written in my letter on 'Amusements'. As a creative art it cannot yet be said to have an existence, although Mr. Wallace composed 'Maritana' in Australia, and plenty of dance-music is manufactured every day.

THE END.